Books by
Jacqueline Jackson

JULIE'S SECRET SLOTH

THE PALEFACE REDSKINS

THE TASTE OF SPRUCE GUM

MISSING MELINDA

CHICKEN TEN THOUSAND

THE GHOST BOAT

SPRING SONG

THE ORCHESTRA MICE

THE ENDLESS PAVEMENT
(*with William Perlmutter*)

TURN NOT PALE, BELOVED SNAIL

Turn Not Pale,
Beloved Snail

Turn Not Pale, Beloved Snail

A Book about Writing among Other Things

Jacqueline Jackson

Little, Brown and Company — Boston – Toronto

SECOND PRINTING

T 11/74

Acknowledgments of permission to reprint excerpted
material appear on Page 233.

LIBRARY OF CONGRESS CATALOGING IN PUBLICATION DATA

Jackson, Jacqueline.
   Turn not pale, beloved snail.
   SUMMARY: Using excerpts from her own writing and that
of her children and other authors, the author suggests a variety
of approaches to learning to write.
   Bibliography: p.
   1. Creative writing — Juvenile literature.
[1. Creative writing] I. Title.
PN187.J3   808'.042   74-12425
ISBN 0-316-45458-8

Designed by Milly Robinson

*Published simultaneously in Canada
by Little, Brown & Company (Canada) Limited*

PRINTED IN THE UNITED STATES OF AMERICA

For J

who

can

fill in

the

blanks

Contents

Introduction: *About This Book*   xi

1   *Catching Woodies*   3

2   *Blind*   15

3   *The Awakened Eye*   24

4   *No Person Does Not Have a Misery*   36

5   *What My Ears Hear*   44

6   *I Didn't Mean to Be Bad*   55

7   *Eavesdrop!*   62

CONTENTS

8   Will You, Won't You Join the Dance?
    (with Some Examples of the Dance)   72

9   The Garlic Sang   81

10   Me Best Thoughts   93

11   Toast that Talks   111

12   When She Was Bad, She Was Horrid   121

13   Mud Between Your Toes   133

14   How (Maybe) to Write a Book   145

15   Warty Bliggins, Smudley Croak:
    The Effanineffable Name   157

16   Gerk   169

17   How (Maybe) to Rewrite a Book — or Anything
    (with Rewriting Revisited and Flat Cat)   188

18   Other People   205

Bibliography   217

Acknowledgments   233

About This Book

Nᴏᴛ ᴀʟʟ ʙᴏᴏᴋs ɴᴇᴇᴅ an introductory note. None of mine up till now have had one, and I always skipped them myself, until I once read one of Walter de la Mare's by mistake, thinking it was the first chapter. But the more I worked on this book, the more I felt I needed to tell the reader something about it and about myself from the very start. So here is an Introduction, which is also sometimes called Author's Note, To the Reader, or, in old books, Dear Reader or Gentle Reader.

This is a book about a lot of things, all clustered around

the idea of writing. I'm writing it because it's the sort of book I wish someone had written for me. From third grade to seventh I filled dozens of notebooks and a fat briefcase with an assortment of stories and poems, but I never saw a book for kids about writing except textbooks. Since then I've seen a few, and a lot more textbooks, for both children and adults, and I haven't found one yet that isn't deadly. I suspect most of them will kill the writer in you, or at least clobber it pretty badly, just as they did to me for a while. In my opinion these books start from the wrong direction, from rules and drudgery rather than from the joy and compulsion of creation.

I'm thinking of you as eight or twelve or fifteen years old, and as a person who is interested in writing, or who might become interested. I'm also thinking of you as twenty and fifty and eighty, for the things I'll be talking about I believe are for people of any age, and it's never too late. I'd just prefer to have said them to you, if you're an adult, when you were sixteen. Or better yet, eleven.

My name is Jacqueline Jackson, and I've published, counting this one, ten books, eleven if you include the one printed in a newspaper when I was ten. Perhaps you've read some of them; you'll find a list if you poke around in the pages before the numbering begins, the part of the book called "the front matter." (A book can refer you all over the place this way, like a treasure hunt. Sometimes the treasure isn't worth it but you never know till you get there.)

In this book, in all my books, a lot of my stories and images are rural and watery, for I grew up on a dairy and hybrid-seed-corn farm in southern Wisconsin, and spent a stretch of summers on a small nearby lake. In the same way, your stories and speech will reflect where you are, or have been, for our deepest impressions settle in our bones when we're little.

My father went to a country school and taught in it for

a year when he was seventeen — he let the kids skate so long on the creek at recess that they all had to stay till suppertime to get their work done — but when I was small the school building had been moved to be a corncrib on the dairy, and we and the neighbor kids went to town in a school bus. Actually, our country district didn't have enough students to fill a bus, so they paid a local taxi firm to squash us all into an old square cab with jump seats. George, his fat cigar stinking, drove us morning and night. This elegant ride made the town kids think we were all millionaires, even though it was the Depression and everybody was as poor as everybody else.

I went to high school and college in the same town, and after graduation married a classmate, Bob Jackson. Right now we both teach in a new university in Illinois. We have four daughters whom we had fun naming: Damaris Lee, called Demi; Megan Trever; Gillian Patricia, pronounced Jillian as in gin, ginger, and Gibraltar; and Jacqueline Elspeth, who is called Elspeth or Beebo, to avoid confusion with me. They all get older every year, so when I refer to them I'll have to give their ages. Right now the older three are getting pretty grown up — Demi's seventeen, Megan's fifteen, Jill's thirteen. Elspeth is often older and wiser than any of us; she's six. Oh, and Frodo is part collie, part German shepherd, and Thorgaut is Megan's big black cat with six white hairs on his chest. I won't go into our confusion of guinea pigs, the Weetles.

What do you do with this book? There aren't any rules. Start anywhere and go anywhere. If you're not interested in writing ("Happiness is showing your calf at the fair, but misery is having to write about it"), maybe you'll find the stories and anecdotes worth reading anyway. If a teacher likes the book, don't let her (or him) shove it down your throat and make lessons out of it, unless that's the way you want to use it. And tell your teacher, if you have to, that the kind of writing this book is about isn't a spelling assignment, or a lesson in grammar or hand-writing or how to make paragraphs. This writing is to get down your good ideas, and what you think and feel inside. Later on, if you like what you've written and want to hand it in to the school newspaper, or post it on the board, or send it in to a magazine, or just keep it for yourself, then is the time to neaten it up and check out the spelling and paragraphs. One problem with school is that if you know you're going to have to rewrite something you often say, "I'll make it perfect the first time — or plenty short —" and that kills it a-borning. The really important thing is first to get it all down without judging whether it's good or bad, and only then to go back, maybe, and rewrite it here and there to make it say what you want even better. If that's as far as you go, that's plenty far.

I suggest you keep your stuff in a notebook or briefcase and call it *My Writing* or *Keep Out*, because you never know when the urge will come to do something fresh with an old idea. Besides, it's fun to look back when you're older, and see what you wrote at an earlier age. Also, when you're grown up, someday one of your kids will be sick and will spend a day rummaging through your briefcase, and will be amazed to realize that you really were a twelve-year-old.

What I'll do in these chapters is give you some suggestions for writing, and these may spark ideas of your own. I'll tell about reading we've liked. Every book I mention I'll put in a list, a bibliography, at the end of the book. Throughout I'll include scraps of my own writing, my children's writing, other kids' writing, and other adult writing. I'll also include a lot of other stuff because that's the way I like to write. Things keep reminding me of things.

And as I've said, what you'll do is write whatever you like, however you like — if you like.

An introduction can also include these final bits: there's a place for the author to claim responsibility for all that's faulty in a book, and ask your forgiveness — so consider your pardon begged. And there's a spot to thank all those who helped, for most books aren't written by the cheese standing alone. So I will end with my list:

My daughters, Damaris, Megan, Gillian, and Elspeth, all writers and critics themselves; my parents, Vera and Ron Dougan, who encouraged me from the crib; Joanne Shaheen of the Rockford Teacher Development Center, who first asked me to work with children on writing in the classroom; Claire Kentzler, friend, excellent editor, and director of the University of Wisconsin WHA School of the Air, over whose radio waves many of these chapters began as part of the program "The Author is You"; Ed and Carol, Chad, Heather, and Sara Dell, who provided fodder for the chapters and also critical readings; ditto Chad, Eva, and Alison Walsh; Eila and Bill Perlmutter, Francis, Greg, and Josie; Mary and Jake, Phoebe and Coby Leed; and Beverly and Jerry Enright. I thank the many children who have shown interest in the sorts of things I've written about here: some of them personal friends, some Wisconsin schoolchildren who have sent their writings to WHA radio station, and some children from schools and book fairs where I have taught or visited. I also thank my students at Sangamon State University, Springfield, Illinois, as well as my colleagues Richard Damashek and Jerry Storm, and my cousin-colleagues Gary Kilarr and Jane DeLawter from Governors State University, for demonstrating that this is a useful book for adults as well as for children. And thanks beyond thanks go to Carole and Joe McHugh, Maurie and Ugo Formigoni, and Kibber and John Miller.

So end of Introduction, and on with woodies!

Turn Not Pale,
Beloved Snail

1

Catching Woodies

I shook and shook the ketchup
But it didn't bloop out
So I stamped the bottle
On the table
And a glob shot up
And made a big red splat
On the ceiling.
"Quick, hold your hamburger under it!"
Daddy said.
"Maybe it'll drip."

— by an anonymous Jackson

IN OUR FAMILY this is what we call a "woody" poem. The name goes back to the first big children's book fair I went to. One thing that's been fun about having books published is that my publishing company began sending me to these fairs. They've changed some, over the years, but at the time I first went, various cities had them, often all in the same week or two, around Children's Book Week in November. Large numbers of children's books were brought in: all the newly published ones that the companies sent, and many of the best books of former years.

These were put on display in libraries, at fairgrounds, or in Chicago at the Museum of Science and Industry, and then kids by the busload came and looked over the books and made lists of the ones they would like to own or have their school libraries order. They sometimes saw a play, or had a program by authors and artists of children's books, which is why I was there.

Some authors and artists considered it a grueling sort of thing and did it only because their publishers wanted them to. It did take a lot of energy to give talks all day and then fly to another city and give talks all the next day, but I enjoyed it and wished my company would send me every year! It was fun to talk with the kids, as well as the teachers, librarians, reviewers, and other people interested in children's books. Parents, too — lots of parents came. It was also revealing to hear and meet the other authors and artists. Some of these were people whose books I'd admired; some whose books I didn't like; and some whose books I'd never even heard of.

One of these latter authors was Mary Neville, whom I met at the Cleveland Book Fair. She was a bright, vivacious person. I liked the way she talked on the programs, and I liked her ideas, but I'd never read a Neville book. So I sneaked off to the display, "Books by Our Guest Authors and Artists," and there one was, a small volume of poems called *Woody and Me.* I've used one at the start of the "Blind" chapter. Here are two others:

PLEASANT STREET

In our town there's a street
Called Pleasant Street.
We don't live on it.
At breakfast, if Woody and me
Are arguing,

4

Mother says,
"Well —
They wouldn't let us
Live on Pleasant Street."

SOCIAL STUDIES

Woody says, "Let's make our soap.
It's easy.
We learned about it
In school."
He told Mother,
"All you do is
Take a barrel.
Bore holes in the sides,
And fill it with straw.
Ashes on top —"

"No," said Mother.

They weren't all this brief. Get the book for yourself and read the long, sad story about the Dick Tracy Detective Squad Car, and its happier sequel.

But are these poems? What is a poem, anyway? These don't sound the way that some people expect poems to sound. They don't rhyme. They don't have a set rhythm pattern. They don't use particularly "poetic" words or "poetic" subjects. But whoever said poems have to rhyme, have set rhythm, and can use only certain kinds of words and subjects? Chad Walsh was my writing prof at Beloit College, and has remained a friend ever since. He sometimes tells his students to visit the local garbage dump and then write a poem on it. This gets them over the idea, fast, that you can only write poems about love, birds, and flowers.

A virtue of a woody is that it's *not* self-consciously poetic. It pops out and there it is. It deals with life's small but memorable moments, and there are many more of these than of the earthshaking ones. A woody tells about the turns and twists of life, the sudden illuminations, the trudges up and slides down, like the Snakes and Ladders game. We all have these at all ages and the material is lying thick around us. But we forget — unless we snatch a pencil and write them down.

Whatever we call these *Woody and Me* bits, they're laid out like poems and they have a sort of rhythm, a speech rhythm. You've heard talk that is as dull and flat as cardboard, and you've heard other talk that's so bright and vivid you enjoy listening to the sound and rhythm of it, as well as the interesting words and ideas in it. Some people talk that way most of the time, and everybody does once in a while, especially little children who haven't been around the world long enough to have soaked up the same old tired way of seeing things and saying things.

Megan came up to me once and said, "Do you know what love is to me? It's when I'm swimming in cold water and suddenly hit a warm spot."

I said, "Megan, that's a poem," and wrote it down:

LOVE
by Megan, age 8

Do you know
What love is
To me?

It's when I'm
Swimming in cold water
And suddenly hit
A warm spot.

6

It wasn't until I read *Woody and Me* that I realized that Megan's was a woody poem, and that we'd been collecting woodies for years. For instance, Demi had limped home from school one day and stood at the door of the camping trailer in our backyard that served as a study for me when we lived in Kent, Ohio. With a little smile in her voice she related the following incident, and then departed for the kitchen and a four-o'clock snack. I grabbed a sheet of paper and wrote down her words as closely as I could remember, stretched out like a poem:

"IH"
Demi at 13

> *Today in gym*
> *I couldn't play because*
> *Of my sprained foot*
> *And so I picked dandelions*
> *And stuck them in the fence to spell "hi"*
> *But the wind kept blowing them out.*
> *Finally I got them to stay*
> *And limped to the outfield*
> *To see how it looked*
> *To the other kids*
> *And it said "ih."*

At supper, she was pleased to see it.
Here's one we call "Cyclops"; I don't remember who said it, maybe Jill:

> *When you put*
> *Your nose*
> *On my nose*
> *And we stare into*
> *Each other's eyes*

Until your eyes
Glide
Into one eye
And so do mine,
Then we're playing
Cyclops.

Or who said this one:

When the dinger dinged
To show the potatoes were done
Nobody was around.
I didn't know what to do
So I set the dinger
For a few more minutes.

These are some of Elspeth's:

DRESSING ON A COLD MORNING

First I get my clothes warm —
Then my clothes get me warm.
Right?
                    — Elspeth, age 4

LISTENING TO MOMMY COMPLAINING

I bet you wish
That picking-up
Meant just sitting around.
Right?
                    — Elspeth, age 4

From now
Until I die
I'll be alive!
                    — Elspeth, age 5

8

FOURTH OF JULY

All over the United States
Fireflies are giving
Their own fireworks
And it doesn't cost a cent!
　　　— Elspeth, age 6

This one is about Elspeth's best friend, Keats, with whom she alternately plays and fights:

I've finally figured out
Why I don't like
Keats.
She takes all the
Importance
Out of you.
　　　— Elspeth, age 6½

"Outrage," by Jill at seven, is self-explanatory — she was in tears of pain and anger:

I was just standing
Under a tree
And a bluejay swooped down
And sat on my head
And pecked me!

Megan's "Revenge" happened on the New York Thruway, at one of those huge awful restaurants. It was crowded and the family had to split up. I was sitting at a counter with Elspeth when Megan, then ten or eleven, came up with a vindictive look on her face, her eyes narrow slits, and blurted out:

When Daddy is old
And wrinkley
And tottery
And hasn't any hair
And hasn't any teeth
I'm going to take him
To a restaurant
And tell him he can spend
Just sixty cents!

I scribbled her words on a napkin with the waitress's order pen.

The other day I found this in the typewriter, abandoned by Demi. I call it "Dull Saturday," and I've drawn a square around it to show you the whole thing goes together and isn't two poems.

Now is the time to say nothing. Nothing. Nothing . . . . . .
I hate weekends.
So do I.
And I.
Also.
Too.
Me.   I HATE WEEKENDS
I.   I HATE WEEKENDS
          I hate them when there is nothing to do.
          But when I can zoom off somewhere
          They're O.K.

And a few weeks ago a friend stayed overnight with our girls. Talie came down to breakfast with these words on her lips:

Megan,
I have sad news for you.

CATCHING WOODIES

You are not
A princess.
All night you slept
With my brush
Under your sleeping bag,
Bristle-side up!

Two more that happened recently:

TO HER FATHER AFTER BICYCLING

When my legs are forty-five
Believe me
They aren't going to be
As forty-five
As yours are!
                        — Megan, age 15

I've only been
To the Children's Zoo
Once
And that was with the school class
And we were all in a bunch
And they told us things
And we couldn't snoop around
For ourselves.
                        — Elspeth, age 6½

That's why I call this "catching" woodies. You're catching a poem rather than sitting down and composing it.
You have to be there with your mitt when the ball comes
down, or with your net when the minnow swims by, or
with your hamburger when the ketchup drips off the
ceiling. You have to have open ears to recognize the
interesting turn of speech, the fresh idea, the amusing
little incident that forms the core of a woody, and then

quickly get it down. You can learn this skill — to tune and sharpen your ears — as you learn many other things, simply by doing it. And to recognize when you yourself say or think a woody, too. Megan could have said, "Do you know what love is to me?" and then written it down herself. Kenneth, a fourth-grade boy, did:

> *Love don't go by what color you are.*
> *Love is something you think about*
> *When you care about someone else.*

My friend Greggie, six or seven, wrote his down too. Like Megan's and Kenneth's it's a "feelings" woody — he was banished to his room for some misdeed and after a while this poem appeared taped to the outside of his closed door:

FOR PARINTS

> *Some things are a little bad.*
> *Some things are a lot bad.*
> *Some things are a little good.*
> *Some things are a lot good.*
> *People in are family,*
> *People in are family,*
> *Avery body likes avery body in there family.*
> *So even if there bad.*
> *Spachly when thir good.*

When we get into thinking and feeling, we can produce another sort of woody besides the sneak-up-and-grab variety. For feeling and thinking don't always deal with the immediate moment. They include a lot of recalling. You can remember the way an incident happened, and write it down. Something made you hold it in memory: there was a little twist to the happening, or something amusing or strange that gave it a niche in your mind. Then something triggered you to recall it, in the present. Here's one I wrote a long time later, about an occurrence in fifth grade. Why have I always remembered it?

COINCIDENCE

> When I was upside down
> Picking up my eraser
> I looked on the underside
> Of my chair.
> There were thirteen wads of gum,
> Some very old.
> But the most remarkable thing
> Was my sister's name
> Written in chalk.
> She must have sat in
> This very chair
> Four years ago.

And one of Jill's friends told me this incident, which a large-flaked snowfall made me remember — though I couldn't recall Debbie's exact words:

> In our class one noon
> Some kids threw
> Wet toilet paper wads
> At the ceiling.
> They stuck!
> Our teacher didn't notice for
> Two whole weeks and then
> Only because a dried one
> Drifted down like a giant snowflake
> During arithmetic.

If you start to write a woody poem from remembering, don't try to make it rhyme. It's usually much better if it doesn't, for the natural, precise word isn't likely to be a rhyming one.

And don't be discouraged if the ketchup of your thought doesn't bloop out immediately. Once it does, there'll probably be enough for several hamburgers. So take your time, think and remember. Have patience. As with the potatoes, set your dinger for a few more minutes.

2

Blind

Woody and I shut
Our eyes and
Groped around
The living room,
Bumping into
Tables and chairs.

We wouldn't let
Ourselves
Open our eyes,
For a while.

A person
Who is really
Blind
Never opens
His eyes.

— "Darkness,"
by Mary Neville

WE HAVE A FRIEND, Edie, about fifteen now, who has been blind from birth. During her early years she went to a special school for the blind in another city, but when it came time to go to middle school she decided to live at home and go to regular "seeing" school. They warned her that it would probably be very difficult and the adjustment hard, but she had a lot of gumption and wanted to try it. And when she moved home for good, the school for the blind did an interesting thing. They sent along with her enough blindfolds for her entire family.

15

What they wanted was for her parents, her brothers and sisters, her grandparents, each to experience for a little while Edie's dark world. Blindfolded, the family would quickly realize certain obvious things. Brothers and sisters would find that stuff strewn all over the floor caused bruises, blood, and broken toys. Everyone would recognize how dependent seeing people are on their eyes, and what a handicap the loss of eyesight is. But if they left the blindfolds on long enough they would begin to learn other, less obvious things.

In a book, *The Treasure of Green Knowe* (called *The Chimneys of Green Knowe* in the English edition), by Lucy Boston, Tolly meets a blind girl, Susan, and later blindfolds himself to see what blindness is like:

Tolly . . . spent the next day playing at being blind. He tried first in the house, feeling his way round the walls, surprised to find how difficult it was to tell that all four walls were not in a straight line but had right-angled corners. . . . The stone walls that were so imposing and certain to sight were gentle and curving to touch, almost warm, to be patted like living creatures. They bulged or sloped away and their edges were blurred or broken off. The many recesses for windows or doors were deeper than the length of his arm, so that if he took his hand off the wall, he was quickly in empty space. And in space, even if it extends only just beyond one's reach, there is nothing to give a direction.

When, after moving cautiously with outstretched hands, he met a piece of furniture, there was pleasure in suddenly recognizing a brass handle or a row of bobbins along the rail of a chair. But they never seemed to be where he had left them. Or sometimes feeling out for the edge of a small table, his hands would meet a vase or candle apparently floating in the air, which was startling, though it only meant that he was holding his hands six inches too high. . . .

He soon found he was quite exhausted, so he took off the blindfold and went off into the garden with Orlando. After some crazy romping he felt better, and then he remembered that blind people had dogs to lead them, so he put Orlando on the lead and put his foot on it while he bandaged his eyes again. Off went Orlando straining like a cart horse. There was grass under his feet, then gravel, then grass again and Tolly very soon had an unreasoning terror of walking over the edge of the earth. Although he dragged back on the lead, it seemed to him that they went like the wind. He had no idea which way he was facing — every stumble left him more uncertain. Where was the wall, where the river or the moat? In a panic he let Orlando go and pulled off his blindfold. He was still on the lawn, facing back to where he had started from — the only direction he had not expected. The world whizzed round him into position again. He flopped into his great-grandmother's garden chair that was there in the sun and lay back to recover his self-confidence.

Later he tries walking again:

Tolly made a careful note of the distance between himself and the tree. I *will* walk there without looking, he decided, and set off with his eyes screwed shut. He walked and walked, stretching out his hands to feel the first beech twigs at the extreme end of the branches. But there was only empty air. He walked farther, as far as it could possibly be — but still only emptiness all round him. And there ought to be ivy underfoot, but there wasn't. Why was it all empty? Had everything disappeared? He opened his eyes and found he had hardly moved from where he started. His many steps had been timorous two-inch shuffles instead of paces. It was silly to be so relieved to find the world was permanent.

At lunch he discussed his experiments with his grandmother:

"It's very tiring not having eyes," he said. "You have to think everything out. But do you know what I have discovered? After my eyes, the most useful things I've got are my feet."

"Not your hands?"

"Well, you can't feel anything unless it's there to feel. There's an awful lot of emptiness. But there's always something under your feet. And they're quite intelligent."

Tolly remained blind long enough to make some subtle discoveries, including the relative intelligence of parts of his body. He discovered his ears were also intelligent, and his skin. He was relying heavily on messages from all over and inside himself that he usually was unaware of, because he had eyes.

Mary Ingalls made those discoveries, too, in *By the Shores of Silver Lake*. You probably know the Little House series, where Laura Ingalls Wilder is writing about her childhood. This book begins when the whole family has just recovered from scarlet fever — but Mary, the oldest girl, has been left blind from it. They are all on a train, moving farther West:

Mary's dress was gray calico with sprays of blue flowers. Her wide-brimmed straw hat had a blue ribbon on it. And under the hat, her poor short hair was held back from her face by a blue ribbon tied around her head. Her lovely blue eyes did not see anything. But she said, "Don't fidget, Carrie, you'll muss your dress."

Laura craned to look at Carrie, sitting beyond Mary. Carrie was small and thin in pink calico, with pink ribbons on her brown braids and her hat. She flushed miserably because Mary found fault with her, and Laura was going to say, "You come over by me, Carrie, and fidget all you want to!"

Just then Mary's face lighted up with joy and she said, "Ma, Laura's fidgeting, too! I can tell she is, without seeing!"

"So she is, Mary," Ma said, and Mary smiled in satisfaction.

Laura was ashamed that in her thoughts she had been cross with Mary. She did not say anything.

If you put yourself in Mary's place, how did she tell that Laura and Carrie were fidgeting? As I sit there, blind in my imagination, waiting for the train to start, the plush-covered seat is jiggling a little, and shifting. This is from the restlessness of my sisters. And they're probably heaving an occasional sigh, or giving little noises of boredom, maybe tapping their teeth, cracking their knuckles, making wriggling sounds. There is a tone of impatience or irritation in their voices. Maybe they jostle me a little. And Mary puts all these things together and realizes to her delight that being in a blind world doesn't mean that she is shut out forever from perception. She can tell that Laura and Carrie are fidgeting! And Laura — Laura also makes a discovery about herself.

For those of us who aren't blind, there's a real fascination with being blind for a while. Look at all the games. Only a few are Blindman's Buff, Poor Pussy, Pin the Tail on the Donkey, and a good one I don't know the name of, but "it" sits outdoors in the center, blindfolded, and one by one the others try to creep up and tag him before he can point and "freeze" the creeper. Whoever tags him gets to be "it." (This is a fine game for autumn, because the leaves crackle.)

Most of us, when we play blind, stay that way just long enough for the game and then with relief rip off the blindfold — though sometimes with the same sobering thought from the woody poem at the start of this chapter: "A person who is really blind never opens his eyes."

It is an interesting and worthwhile experience, and especially valuable for a writer, to be blind for more than just a few moments. It will give you quite a lot to write about, and it will also reveal some pretty interesting things about yourself and other people, and the world.

You might try shutting your eyes after you read this paragraph. Keep them shut, no peeking, long enough for something else to begin to take place. What do you become aware of? What sounds are going on? Are you conscious of the floor under your feet? A desk under your fingers? The paper of this book, the binding? Have you ever noticed the feel of a book, the texture of its pages, its smell?

Try writing down, in detail, what you discovered in this brief blindness.

Then carry the experiment still further, for a longer time, in different places. Walk, indoors and out, like Tolly did. Stop and listen. Demi's ninth-grade science teacher took a small group of students and parents out into a woods at night, and each parent and child shared a blanket. We weren't blindfolded for it was pitch-dark, but we lay, in utter silence, for an hour. At first I could hear only one loud insistent insect, a steady sort of chirping, and I listened to it for a long time before I realized that there was a whole background of lesser insect noises that I hadn't heard at all. After turning my attention for a while to these, and trying to differentiate between them, I suddenly realized that the loud insect which had first attracted me had quieted down —not actually, but my ears had tuned him out and were now tuning in the other insects exclusively. This taught me something about my own hearing: while I was concentrating on one sound I would lose another.

The next step in increasing listening awareness might be to see if one can hear in total, at least for short times: tune in everything. And then there are the awarenesses of the other senses. The touch of the wind. The smell of pine and earth. Or, of hot exhaust — for the science teacher on another night took our same group downtown and we sat, this time blindfolded, at a bus stop, experiencing the city for contrast. Cars and buses came and went; so did people. A few lingered, loudly curious about this peculiar group, but a policeman had been assigned to take care of us, and didn't let anyone kick us to see if we were alive.

Then, if you can, be blindfolded for a whole day. I read in a magazine about how a teacher taped cotton pads over some students' eyes so that no glimmer of light could get in. Those who volunteered for this experience stayed blind for several days, even a week. What was the teacher hoping to teach them? And what did they learn?

It's the sustained experience that will be most valuable. You'll become increasingly aware, not only of how you perceive things outwardly, but of what your inner self is like. Do you feel terror? Panic? Calm? Detachment? What sorts of things do you think about? You're more "with" yourself — you're less distracted by externals. You can't pick up a newspaper and read anything at all to keep yourself from thinking.

And when you finally take off your blindfold, what do you see? What are your feelings? In Chaim Potok's The Chosen, Reuven has an eye injury which may blind him permanently. When the bandages are removed, he does have vision — but because of his experience he sees in a different way than he ever has before: "The hydrangea bush — or snowball bush, as we called it — on our lawn glowed in the sunlight, and I stared at it. I had never really paid any attention to it before. Now it seemed suddenly luminous and alive." Will any of the perceptions and abilities and intelligences you discovered when you were blind linger on with you into a new way of seeing?

A person who is really blind will know a lot of these things already. He will never be able to do certain jobs that require eyes — drive a car, study through a telescope or microscope. But there are many things he can do as well as or better than sighted people. One of these is to write.

Tradition says that one of the greatest poets of all time, Homer, who wrote the story of Troy and the wanderings of Ulysses in the *Iliad* and the *Odyssey,* was blind. The British poet John Milton wrote *Paradise Lost* after he was blind. Helen Keller was both deaf and blind from the age of two, yet she became a very fine writer. You've perhaps read books about her, and seen the play and movie *The Miracle Worker;* now read her autobiography, *The Story of My Life.* And James Thurber, who wrote children's and adult books, told some pretty funny and poignant stories about his own near-blind eyesight.

Edie, our blind friend, is a writer, and she brought some of her stories to our house. We sat around the dining room table reading aloud. After a little while, Demi remarked that practically all of Edie's writing was conversation and other things that came to her through her ears. Demi ran and got her own journal, and compared some of her passages with Edie's. Almost all Demi's perceptions came through her eyes. They were excellent observations, but she was largely lacking the intelligence of the ears. Both girls, we noticed, didn't record much perception through their other senses — their noses, tongues, and skins. After they realized this, they began to include more of these awarenesses in their writings.

I said that these blindness games will be valuable to you as a writer. But their main value to you can be in another way. For writing doesn't depend as much on the images you see with your eyes, or the sounds you hear with your ears, as it does on your "inner eye," your "inner ear," the understandings you have inside you that you glean from all your senses, including your heart. The more you learn about your own inners, the deeper understanding you will have about yourself and about everybody. You'll be seeing with your heart, and then if you write it down, fine. The writing will be the richer. But the writing's not the most important thing in the world. The understanding is.

3

The Awakened Eye

Shivering, Marcy sat cross-legged on the stump at the top of the hill. The late-afternoon sun stretched her shadow before her, her head spilling over the hill. She found it sitting like the Cheshire cat in a tree half-way down.

. . . Her finger tips were puckered and the nails blue, and her arms were stippled with goose bumps. Underneath her the stump slowly gave off its stored-up heat. The sun penetrated her back. She wrung out a trickling braid. Like a blotter, the stump absorbed the water down thousands of tiny cracks, and turned black.

A motion on the path caught her eye. A wasp was crawling out of a hole! Her wings, like last year's jacket, didn't cover her narrow waist and fat round abdomen, which was shiny black with an orange band. . . .

— From *The Paleface Redskins*

WHEN EDIE, THE BLIND FRIEND I told you about in the last chapter, decided to leave her special school and go to a regular seventh grade, her mother commented, "Most people who have eyes don't see very well."

Most of us are like horses with blinders on. That's an image that may not mean much to you — I rarely see a workhorse myself, these days. But when I was small, the teams on the farm — old Bess and Barney, Mac and Jenny — had tabs on their harness that didn't cover their eyes but kept them from having any side vision. This was so they'd not notice each other and other distractions, but keep their minds on the furrow ahead and no frisky business. And since horses' eyes are set so that they see mostly to the side (like cows and giraffes, all grass-eaters, and the victims of lions and other animals of prey), they can't have seen very much at all.

Growing up, you would think, is a process of the world gradually opening up to us, like a crescendo in music, starting small from when we are born and then spreading wider and wider. But somewhere along the line we begin to close in again so that we start cutting off the world. We don't hear as much, we don't see as much, we don't feel as much. There are lots of reasons for this, some necessary, but it's too bad that we keep limiting ourselves in area after area more than we need to.

When I was nine or ten we were driving once through the countryside. My father glanced into the back seat and discovered that all four of us, as usual, were sitting with our noses inside of books. I guess I didn't tell you in the introduction: I'm the third of four — Joan, Patty, Jackie, Craig — all of us close in age. Read *Palefaces* and *Ghost Boat*; that's us, more or less. Well, my father is a reader, but he's also a watcher and he said, irritated, "Why don't you kids look out the window, why don't you see what's going on around you? I'll give you a dime for every pheasant you spot, and a nickel for every partridge and a penny for every quail." Well, that raised our noses in a hurry, and we began looking for pheasants. A dime was worth more then; remember it was the Depression.

I think this was one of the richest things my father ever did for us, and I don't mean the money. What he wanted was for us to sharpen our eyes. We watched for pheasants from then on — we didn't much bother with the small peanuts — and began to find them everywhere, usually well camouflaged in the weedy ditches and thickets. In the process we began to see everything else, too. The game ended when we discovered, like Aladdin and his treasure cave, that there was a mother pheasant and her numerous chicks living in our lane. So every morning when we ran to catch the school taxi, and every evening when we walked back, we gleefully counted the entire family. Daddy's rules didn't say you couldn't use the same pheasant twice, and we felt eight hours was a fair interval for spotting. At the end of the week of this bonanza discovery we presented our enormous bills. My father paid up gallantly but decided that we'd developed the desired skill and so didn't need to be bribed to pursue it any further. I can still spot a pheasant two fields away, and do, automatically. And my ears always select, out of myriad other noises, a pheasant's distinctive "berk-berk" call.

My father, a few years back, gave a similar experience to two of his grandchildren, my nieces Jackie Jo and Steffie. While driving along another country road he said, "Keep your eyes peeled and let me know if you see anything of uncommon interest." Almost immediately Jackie Jo said, "What's that great big bird?" Well, it wasn't any pheasant, but over on the horizon, circling down and landing in the treetops, *was* a large bird. My father stopped and trained his bird glasses on it (never go anywhere without your bird glasses) and it was a great blue heron. Not just one, either; another flew in and landed, and then another one. Daddy said, "Well, I guess we'd better investigate what's going on over there." So the three of them tramped across a couple of fields and through a woods to a clearing in the middle of it, ringed with tall dead trees, and stood gaping up at dozens of brush-pile nests with great blue heron babies sitting in them, with their necks a yard long and their beaks a foot, and fifty or sixty father and mother birds wheeling in on the high wind, bringing them frogs and other dainties and saying *gronk*. It was a great blue

heron rookery, and nobody knew it was there except the
farmer who owned the land and he wasn't talking. The
local bird club knows now, but otherwise it's still a secret.
Oh, Steffie spotted something that day, too; a great
horned owl.

And a recent experience of mine and Elspeth's — we
were walking along a medium-traveled sidewalk in downtown Springfield, in broad daylight, when Elspeth said,
"Look, there's a bat." Sure enough, hanging upside down
by the claws, at her eye level, was a small brown bat,
blending in well with the coarse red-brown bricks of the
bank exterior it was clinging to. I was impressed with
Elspeth's eyesight, but we were both worried about the
bat. Would it be safe there, in plain view? We contem-
plated moving it around the corner to a less conspicuous
place, but had some reservations. Could we hitch it back
on so it'd stick? What if it woke and flew to some daylight
fate? Or it might bite, and since bats are sometimes rabid
we'd have to have it killed to find out.

Some people were coming along and an idea struck me.
"Let's stand over by the parked cars," I said, "and see if
anybody notices." So we retreated to the curb. We appeared to fuss with a meter but secretly watched while a
couple, then a group, then a few singletons, then another
group passed the bat. Not a single person showed any sign
of sighting it! So we left with lightened hearts. We knew
the bat was safe.

Most of us not only don't peel our eyes, but when we
do see something we don't see it very accurately. One of
the best ways of eye-sharpening is to draw something
while looking at it. If you try to draw a foot, or how a
head is set on a neck, or, heaven forbid, an ear from
memory, unless you're very unusual you'll find that you've
never really *observed* those things. If you then study them
closely, draw (don't worry about how "good" a likeness

you make!), and at a later time draw again from memory, you'll have something stored up and should do very much better. When I illustrated *Palefaces* and *Ghost Boat* I realized time and again that I didn't really know in my bones how the curve of a shoulder went, or the turn of a dog's leg, until I went and looked.

You might think sketching is a tame occupation, but it can have its moments of drama. I was once checking out a drawing of goats when a big bearded billy thrust his head through the fence, snatched my picture, and gave it several good chomps before I managed to force his jaws open and get it back.

Another eye-peeler is to play vision games. Here I want to recommend a fine book whose title I stole for this chapter, *The Awakened Eye*, by Ross Parmenter. Ross has a whole chapter of these activities. One of his suggestions is to try seeing from all sorts of different viewpoints; for instance, bend down and look through your legs to see the world backwards and upside down. It makes things leap into a different focus from your usual one — unless you're a football center!

Or take a piece of paper, make a pinhole, and look at the world through that minuscule opening. Then there's a kind of kaleidoscope that has mirrors at the end and takes the outside world for its patterns rather than little things falling around inside. I'm sure there's a special name for it, but if you look through this "kaleidoscopy" instrument, it will take a piece of curtain or a segment of a person's face and repeat it six or eight times in a design so that you forget what it *is*, in the way you usually see it, but are intensely aware of the colors, the shapes, the lights and darks, the textures. Then when you look back at the object, you see it in a renewed, fresh way.

This is true also for seeing parts of a whole in other ways. If you were to study a feather under the microscope, or in enlarged drawings in a book, and discover the way each individual barb hooks into the next one, with little barbules and still smaller barbicels, then when you see the whole feather again it has more meaning for you because you better understand its structure. None of us will ever see the moon the same way again, because now we have a double vision: as it is up there in the sky, and as the astronauts see a lunar landscape.

Another game Ross mentions — I use his first name because he's an old friend; he uses the story of my father and the pheasants in *his* book! — is one you might be familiar with, the old game of putting objects on a tray, showing everyone, and taking the tray away. You then all see how many objects you can remember. Another friend, Louisa Liske, plays this game with her kindergartners. But she doesn't just put a nut on the tray; she puts on a hickory nut, a pecan, a black walnut, a buckeye. She doesn't just put on a leaf; she puts on an oak leaf, a maple, an elm, a locust.

Our girls love Camouflage. Ahead of time, someone hides a whole lot of things in plain sight but in unexpected places, such as a knife in a vase of flowers along with the stems, or — the best stumper we ever had — a breakfast Cheerio at eye level on a nail against the unpainted wall of our summer cottage. Everyone is given a list of the camouflaged items, and the winner is the one who spots them all first.

Studying pictures is another way of increasing awareness. We have artist friends who have files of pictures that they've gathered over the years, from magazines, postcards, photographs. Then if *they* need to draw a goat they can go to "Animals" (or "Goats" if their files are large and well organized) and riffle through their collection. This will give them a starting place, a toehold for drawing. A reminder of things goatish.

A writer needs a file of pictures, too; a real file, possibly, but more important, a mind-file, a mind-bank. When you're writing it's impossible to go see everything afresh. We can't be reliving everything all the time. If you've stored up a whole lot of visual images you can describe a face, a look, a scene, without having to see it at that very moment. You don't watch a house burn down very often (unless you're a fireman) and you probably can't produce one at the time you want to describe it (unless you're an arsonist). But if you've ever seen one, there are going to be vivid things you've stored in your memory — the blackness of the weeds silhouetted against the burning structure, the second-floor bathtub and toilet left balanced on their pipes when the floors and walls collapse.

We save these things unconsciously, as I saved a picture of the setting sun and used it in *Palefaces*: "White Feather's face as she squatted by the fire was as red as the sun that was resting like a squashed tomato on the rim of the hill behind the swamp." I don't recall ever deliberately noticing that close to the earth the sun appears flattened on top and bottom like a pressed balloon — an effect that has something to do with looking through dense air layers — yet when I saw a red globe setting in my mind, there it was, slightly flat. We can also save visual images consciously. I have observed and said, "I will remember this sight," and stored it away in my mind-bank.

I'm not sure all writers write this way, but I think — and write — by eye and not by words. I realized this at a party when I was in graduate school, and was intrigued and astounded as we all are when we make profound self-discoveries. We played a game called Association. Everyone put the same word at the top of a sheet of paper. Then we each wrote what word that word reminded us of, and the next word, for twenty words, whereupon we read our lists out loud. It was interesting to see what divergent paths people's minds took, how starting out with "watermelon" one person could end up with Hoyle's theory of the constant creation of the universe, or another with the weather in Opelika, Alabama.

Everybody but me. I discovered my mind didn't work that way. I *saw* a watermelon in my mind, and no particular word popped in to accompany it. I mentally had to describe a watermelon and scenes where I had experienced watermelons, and then arbitrarily choose a word from that description. Shall it be *rind? Seeds? Boat,* from the time we ate a warm melon in a rowboat? *Pink,* or *whiskers,* from the time I fed my pet goat a piece of watermelon and she ended up with delicate pink-fringed lips? Everyone else was writing briskly, and when their twenty words were finished I only had five or six, and a terrible case of frustration. But I learned that when I think, I think in pictures before words, and then I describe the picture as completely as I can, and somewhere along the way the sounds, smells, and so on, float into it and get described, too, for these are also part of the picture. This is like seeing a movie for the first time. In the rewrite, I run the movie through a second or even a third time (actually it's more like *living* a movie through, since I put myself into it) and this time I notice things overlooked the first time — sharper details, more conversations, directions I might have gone and still can. It builds on the first time.

In the first writing of *Palefaces* I said, "White Feather slopped soup into the bowls and served bacon with the twig." The second time I saw the bacon more clearly: ". . . served bacon with the twig, as though lifting angleworms from a bait can." The reader will know that this particular bacon must be a little limp. And knowing this helps, because a crisp piece of bacon would present problems balanced on a twig, and the reader, if he makes the crisp picture for himself, might be distracted from the story.

I also change to more accurate words. Often the right

word isn't there at the first writing. Sometimes I leave a blank and come back later. But that makes a lot of empty spaces, so I usually put down a word, in parentheses, which is almost the right one; sometimes I even mark it "ww," for wrong word, but, you know, let's get on with it, the first telling, the initial impetus. Later the word will come, or I'll go seek it from other persons or books or dictionaries.

So for me, at least, it's important to have a mind-bank filled with a lot of pictures, a lot of details, for these are what I base my writing on and are the solid ground for imaginary scenes. Or maybe I just write this way because I'm lucky enough to have a lot of mind-pictures.

I mentioned books. A valuable aid to better seeing is reading the books of authors who see. Their keen perceptions help us to be more acute. This helps us to be better writers and also increases our enjoyment of living in general. We have more understanding of the world by getting other points of view. I don't think that reading is any substitution for the actual looking, but reading will help us to look with clearer vision. The two feed each other: we look and then we read; we read and then we look. And a book, of course, will often let us see things we'd never see otherwise, things out of our time and place. We can't all climb Mount Everest or examine the nostrils of a llama. But we can gain skill in learning to describe by studying those who do it well no matter what their scene.

Our daughter Jill is such a reader that I thought she never saw anything except bookprint. I quit worrying when I found that when she did pry herself loose, she observed exceptionally well. The other summer, for instance, she asked me if I knew that there were two varieties of willow trees in the thicket around her grandpa's pond. When I said no, she showed me that a willow leaf from one variety came right up to the twig and stopped, whereas on the other variety the end of the leaf encircled the twig like a tiny ruff. A casual look would declare them identical. For all my years of crouching in willow thickets it had never occurred to me to compare the way the leaves are attached. I wonder how much Jill's reading has sharpened her vision? I would bet a lot.

As for specific books, I could name a hundred. *The Wind in the Willows* sees, and *Charlotte's Web*. Harriet, the spy, is training herself to see:

MISS WHITEHEAD'S FEET LOOK LARGER THIS YEAR. MISS WHITEHEAD HAS BUCK TEETH, THIN HAIR, FEET LIKE SKIS, AND A VERY LONG HANGING STOMACH. OLE GOLLY SAYS DESCRIPTION IS GOOD FOR THE SOUL AND CLEARS THE BRAIN LIKE A LAXATIVE. THAT SHOULD TAKE CARE OF MISS WHITEHEAD.

Theodore Taylor sees, in *The Cay*, and William Mayne in all his books, but most enjoyably for me in *A Swarm in May*. Lucy Boston, in *The River at Green Knowe*, sees water so powerfully that at one point I couldn't go on but had to close my eyes and let the water wash over me.

There are writing ways to develop our seeing skills. Make some simple lists of what you see and describe things as freshly and differently as you can. Things that have struck you. Your lists can be turned into poetry very easily, for poetry is a sort of condensed seeing. The descriptions don't need to be long, just a flash. I found in Demi's journal, "Birds sit puffed like soup bowls on the telephone wires," and on another page, "A brilliant discovery: one would expect pomegranates to stain red, but my fingers are the color of tarnish on bronze."

Another way is really to look at something, even something quite ordinary, such as your hand, and see if you can write a whole page, two pages, describing it. What about those fine little wrinkles — do they remind you of anything? — the pattern of the bones, the hairs, the look of the palm as compared to the back? And what about what your hand means to you, what you can do with it? That's when you get into the depths of your hand, seeing "into" it. Those opposed thumbs of ours, anthropologists say, have been very important to our development as human creatures. Do you have any special feeling for your thumbs?

Study other things. I'm fond of ears. Try a human ear, a dog's ear, a cat's ear. Ever notice that funny little pocket on the side of a cat's ear? I like tongues, too. A cat's tongue and a dog's tongue are quite different. The roof of a dog's mouth bears investigation, also a cat's paw, a dog's paw. Or maybe you don't have animals. Some fourth-graders were taken by their teacher to look at winter weeds and one wrote, "Broken spears like rabbit ears poking through the snow." Brief, but with real feeling. Another wrote, "Starched weeds, parched weeds, rubbing one another."

For a story, you could write out a time when you actually, really *saw* something you'd been looking at for years, such as your own face. Why did you suddenly see it as if for the first time? Another idea: Helen Keller has a book, *Three Days to See.* I've not been able to find it, but the title suggests a boy we knew in college who, when he was fourteen, had to have an operation that saved his life but destroyed his eyesight. If you only had three days, or three weeks, to see, what sort of things would you look at? Seek out? Store up in your memory bank for the rest of your life?

There's a final point I'd like to make, which is in Ross's book. He says he thinks the thing that makes us the poorest lookers, why we see so little, is that we don't take time. In this country especially we rush, rush, rush, and we feel we have to be busy or we're not being useful. But to sit and look into a fire, or at moving water, or at the stars, or at somebody's face, or at an anthill — these things are very important to our souls. Children know this instinctively. Some grown-ups, like Ole Golly, haven't forgotten it, but most of us as we grow older have this squeezed out of us by adult pressures to *accomplish*. As if taking in these impressions isn't accomplishing something, and something absolutely vital!

The thing that will help our writing most, as well as our souls, is to begin to take time for these sorts of activities. To become real watchers. To look again and again and again until what we see is soaked in and is *there*. Forever. To recognize that our eyes have been asleep, and start awakening them.

4

No Person
Does Not Have a Misery

"Misery is when you put a dime in the pop machine and the pop comes out but the cup doesn't drop down, and after the pop stops, down drops the cup."

"Misery is laughing so hard you wet your pants."

"Misery is having to kiss the hem of a skirt in a play."

You're probably as familiar with Linus and Lucy, Charlie Brown, Pigpen, Snoopy, Schroeder — all the Peanuts characters — as you are with the kids in the next block. And you've probably read not only Charles Schulz's comic strips about them, but also his "concept" books — books that take an idea or concept and describe it from all sorts of directions. "Happiness Is a Warm Puppy." "Security Is a Thumb and a Blanket."

Shortly after the first of these came out, a little book was published called *Misery*, by Susan Heller. "Misery is when you spend your last ten cents on a Good Humor and it falls off the stick." "Misery is when you are the fattest kid in the class and it's time to go to the nurse's office to be measured and weighed." "Misery is when it's Halloween and you are a ballerina and your mother makes you wear a coat and nobody can see your costume." "Misery is when you are riding in a car and everyone smells dog doody and you discover it's on *your* shoes." "Misery is when you bring the class hamster home for the weekend and it disappears into a mouse hole."

Our family had this *Misery* book with us, along with thirty other library books, on a camping trip. One evening while we were sitting with friends around the campfire and roasting marshmallows Megan, then about nine, studied a boiling blob on a log and remarked ruefully, "Misery is when the last marshmallow falls off your stick into the fire."

That got us going. Demi said, "Misery is seeing a big fat spider walk across your toothbrush," and Jill, "Misery is having to go to the bathroom in the woods and there are fifty million mosquitos." My contribution was, "Misery is when in the middle of a camping trip your nine-month baby refuses all baby food and wants only hot dogs." For a while the miseries centered around camping miseries, but then we gradually found ourselves — adults and kids alike — going into the past for miseries: "Misery is when you have warts on your hands and you play circle games at recess, and you know that nobody wants to stand next to you."

I found myself dredging up buried miseries that were so deep and personal that I'd never had the courage to tell them to anybody before, and I realized the others were doing the same. It was easy to tell our own miserable experiences in this anonymous way, in the midst of a good-humored and sympathetic gathering. Each of us was trying to outdo the others in miseries, as if to say, "Sure, that was pretty miserable all right, but wait till you hear *this* one!"

For me this telling was a window into the secret spots of my children, framing unhappy experiences that I'd never known about, or if I had, that I hadn't realized. In fact, I was sometimes the cause of them! I was allowed to see from the child's point of view what before I'd only seen from the mother's, or not even seen at all. This same window revealed my husband and our friends. I also gave everybody a window to myself, one that showed both my childhood miseries and my grown-up ones.

We must have sat there for two hours, cheerfully recalling more and more wretched miseries while we poked sticks into the glowing embers of the fire. It was a remarkable time of warmth and depth, of real communication. Everybody sensed it. Later I thought, why didn't we talk about "Happiness Is," or "Security Is"? Why just "Misery Is"?

I thought of Alison, a friend who's in college now but who was four when a group of us, all ages, were discussing the good and the bad, whether you remember one more than the other. Somebody asked Alison's opinion and without a second's hesitation she declared, "The *bad!* Becky squashed my bug!"

Do we really remember the bad more than the good, the miseries more than the happinesses? Or is it that we remember the *details* of the miseries? I had a happy childhood on the whole, and especially happy were the seven summers we spent at a small lake in southern Wisconsin. Yet when it comes to remembering specific moments of emotion, it's usually the more traumatic that I recall in sharp picture. The happiness is diffused over all those summers in a sort of blissful glow, but I can still feel the horror and guilt, and see the black soot on my father's silver baby mug after I used it to brew acorn tea, and thought I'd ruined it. And what about that acute discomfort when I, a lofty lake dweller, decided to honor the Girl Scouts at their camp with a social call, and then found they absolutely ignored me? And the helpless outrage I felt when I was hauled, struggling, crying, and dripping, into the rowboat by Paul, my older cousin? He was tending us for the day and I'd gotten mad and screamed, "I'm leaving! I'm going to swim across the lake!" and I'd stomped down to the dock, flung myself in, clothes and all, and struck out for the far shore. Even as I write this, I can see Paul's fiendish grin, and the flaky paint on those rowboat gunnels, and the bilgy water in the boat bottom. Also those flabby Girl Scouts sprawled in their tents reading comic books and popping bubble gum. The strong emotion of each specific horror has frozen the whole thing into a picture, including, sometimes, the actual words someone spoke.

Is this true for you? Do you remember the miseries more clearly than the happinesses? Can you remember one, from this morning, or last week, or last year, that is especially miserable and especially vivid?

A list is a good place to begin. See how many you can get. You don't need to limit yourself to calling them just miseries, either. There are lots of forms of misery, and you might be more explicit:

"Panic is when you're in a big crowded department store and you find out the person you've been following isn't your mother."

"Boredom is having no one to fight with you."

"Disaster is overflowing your friend's toilet!"

You might even let a happiness creep in, if you recall a clear one:

"Contentment is the cat under the covers at the foot of your bed. You can feel her purring with your toes."

"Joy is visiting your mother in the hospital and the operation has turned out OK."

Then, when you have a good strong list of miseries and other emotions (and not just top-of-the-head ones; go for those deep-down-pit-of-the-stomach ones) you have a gold mine for writing a story. For writing lots of stories. The lists are fun, but the stories are more fun, for now you take the feeling that you wrote with the most relish ("Satisfaction is hitting my brother over the head with an egg"), or the most grief ("Misery is when you get a little baby sister. Then you are no more longer thought of"), or the most quaking of your innards ("Misery is not being able to find your paper and you know you did it," or "Misery is when the teacher makes you write a note to your parents"), and you think it through. You go from the bare bone, the spark of the idea, to details about the where and how, and the more of these the better. What caused you to remember that misery, that feeling? How did it start? What happened? How did people look, speak, *feel?* How did you look, speak, *feel?* And how did it end — if it has?

I wish the boy who wrote the "kissing the hem of the dress" misery had given us the whole story: I imagine an old-fashioned play, full skirts, maybe Columbus being grateful to Queen Isabella, and the horrible moment coming up when the fellow playing Columbus has to drop to his velvet knee and kiss the sweeping skirt. Imagine the suppressed snickers of the rest of the class! The haughty queen is probably a girl he either likes or doesn't like, but either way is excruciating! And don't think it isn't just as bad for her. I once refused to be a queen in a play, because

I had to say "Yes, my darling" to the king, and take his hand.

Demi wrote out a list of embarrassments the other day. I enjoyed particularly the first one because it was a recent incident that I was part of. She said, "Embarrassment is when you have been stealthily trailing your family through the woods and you suddenly realize that your mother has been trailing you." There it is, just a little sentence and you get the picture, but I think that it would be an interesting story for Demi to write up in detail. She could tell her feelings, why she abandoned her family when they were out hiking together in the woods, why she hung behind until they'd gotten so far ahead that they were no longer in sight. Why, when they called her, she didn't respond. Why, instead, she stood behind a tree. What were her thoughts? We all have a need to be by ourselves. One of my scorns at that lake I've mentioned was the Girl Scout Camp, where the scouts were always, it seemed to me, doing things in great mobs. They would walk around the lake in a line that would take five minutes to go past our cottage. I used to think to myself, "What can anybody see on a hike with a hundred other people? Anything worth seeing gets trampled or scared away before you get there." Demi probably had some of these same feelings: "I'm out here in the woods, I want to be alone, I don't want to be with my family, I'm always with my family." She also wanted us to worry about her a little, maybe, to cause us a little inconvenience. When she didn't catch up, I doubled back to speed her up. I went stealthily myself, because I suspected she was feeling this way. When I finally spotted her I hid behind a tree and allowed her to come along past me. She would pause; examine oak bolls or mushrooms; sometimes just stand vacantly, with thoughts moving behind her eyes. Her attention would be caught by noises, and her head would swivel up or around.

She watched the path to be sure she was safe from the view of the family tramping noisily far ahead. I nearly laughed out loud, spying on Demi as she was spying on us. And then she spotted me!

There are two stories here, actually. Maybe you noticed that I switched midway from imagining Demi's thoughts to telling my own. She and I could each write our own story.

If you write out your misery tales you may find some benefits besides the fun of doing it, and having a good yarn to share when you're through. There were certain things that bothered me terribly when I was little, yet when I was older I looked back and thought, "That wasn't so awful — why did I agonize so?" And yet I had, waking in a cold sweat in the night. By seeing now that something really wasn't so horrible then, I sometimes can see my present miseries in more perspective. Maybe these, too, aren't quite so bad as I think.

Or, looking back, when I realize, "If I'd only tried to explain to my teacher, she might have understood," I make the leap of thought, "Perhaps there's some action I can take on this misery right now that will diminish it."

Of course, no misery is inconsequential when you're having it, whether you're four or fourteen or forty. What's miserable to a four-year-old is really miserable by his standards, and often by anybody's. It's always miserable to be kicked around, humiliated, or misunderstood. And it can really be a lot worse at four: you haven't the words to explain, or you don't understand as well, yourself. You aren't old enough, for instance, to realize someone's clobbering you because someone just clobbered him and he can't clobber back. (If understanding the *why* of a clobber makes it feel any better.) And too often people simply don't listen or understand, at any age. Also, at four you are just beginning to build up an inner callus (the way the soles of your feet harden from going barefoot), that allows you to shrug hurts off. You're more easily hurt because you haven't gotten used to hurts. That's one reason early childhood miseries are so vivid.

And then there are real solid miseries that can't be changed: "Misery is when your worst sister dies, even though you never liked her." Even these may be softened by writing them out.

Finally, when you are writing down your misery stories and sharing the miseries of others, you can't help but realize what a fourth-grader named Theresa wrote. "Misery is when you do not like something or someone. Every person has a misery. No person does not have a misery."

You. Me. Grandparents. Teachers. Little brothers. You'll come to understand people better, that we're all in together on the joys and miseries of humankind. And to know this — that we're not alone — helps us to live with misery. Real misery.

5

What My Ears Hear

CHADDIE WAS EXCITEDLY telling about something he'd heard. His friend interrupted. "You didn't hear that," he said, and began to give his own account of the affair. Whereupon Chaddie interrupted Johnny and said in a voice dripping with scorn, "*Your* ears can't hear what *my* ears hear!"

You know, it's true when you think about it. What Chaddie was saying, with four-year-old wisdom, was that what comes to him through his ears gets sent to his brain in a different way than what comes into Johnny's ears, so that both of them can be in the same spot, ears exposed to the some noises, yet they will be getting different messages. This is true of all our senses, and is one of the marvelous things about being human. We're all alike, yet we are each absolutely unique. My ears can't hear what your ears hear.

I read a book about a man, deaf from a childhood accident, who suddenly, through another accident, regained his hearing. He lay in his hospital bed in a torment of confusion because the world was so noisy, until his brain adjusted to screening out certain sounds and he developed a selective pattern to his hearing.

In the "Blind" chapter I mentioned selective listening, and in "Awakened Eye" how my own ears are alert to a pheasant's cry. I also hear mourning doves; once I was standing on the steps of a city auditorium during a concert intermission and said aloud, amid the traffic and chatter, "There's a mourning dove." A strange man alongside said, "You heard that, too? I thought I was the only one who ever heard mourning doves," and we had a pleasant moment of kinship. Yet there were certainly other birds — and sounds — we were both tuning out.

Similar examples are easy to find. My sister and I shared a room, growing up, and one night she became very sick. I slept through the whole commotion — parents, doctor, and all. But when my own girls were small, my ears became tuned to hear them if they cried, and I'd wake up quickly.

If you're like Jill, and I was this way, too, you are absolutely earless when you're lost in a book. When your brain is busy elsewhere, you don't hear. And book or not, I bet you also tune out your mother asking you to do something. No wonder we mothers nag!

Babies cover a tremendous range of different sounds in their babbling. Gradually, by hearing the language around them, they select out of their own noises the ones that have meaning, and discard the others, so that they eventually are no longer capable of making many of the sounds they earlier could, and no longer hear the nuances of difference, either. This is probably why they can't make the sounds; the tongue follows the ear. To learn to imitate the sounds of a foreign language late in life is very difficult, the more so the farther removed the language is from the familiar sounds of one's own tongue. For instance, the clicks and pops of Bantu from English. This is a basic reason why it's good to learn other languages very young. Our ears haven't yet solidified, calcified.

We're all selective listeners, and I guess have to be, but most of us, I feel, select too little, and don't vary our selection from time to time, don't turn the knob. It's one of those diminuendos of life, where we begin early to close ourselves off, and to be aware of less and less. Our protection becomes a handicap, and we lose a vast wealth without realizing it.

How can we expand our ears and add new "hear" experiences to our consciousness? We'll be better writers for it, and we'll also find more delight in being alive, if we can tap this wealth.

A first step is to realize how poorly we listen, by consciously listening. This was at least part of what Demi's biology teacher was aiming at, when he took us to the woods and then to the street corner. Tolly does it, eyes shut, in *Treasure of Green Knowe:*

> "Now I'll lie here and listen to what Susan heard," he thought, and at once realized how much wind there was, and how big, telltale, and friendly. It bumped into and passed round sheds; it crossed the gravel, bowling protesting dead leaves before it. It made a different sound in each tree, in some like the sea, in others like fretted tissue paper. How it whirled the yew branches about! Tolly could imagine the clouds moving like ships under full sail, but Susan would know nothing about clouds or sky, and never could.

But surely somehow she would feel the *size* of the wind? She could hear it approach from far away and the immense hubbub of its passing. The birds were trying to sing, because it was March, but the song was interrupted, jerked out of their throats as they were tossed off the branches by the wind and flew with an extra flutter that reminded Tolly of rowing in rough water. He heard the branches of two trees that leaned against each other squeaking and groaning like an overloaded cart. He heard the church clock strike one, and Boggis slipped past on his bicycle almost as quietly as an owl. The sound was so slight he opened his eyes to see if he had guessed right. . . .

Like Tolly, try the "Blindness" games again, concentrating on your ears. Seek out varied places, and listen to the character of sound. Is there noise? How many strands can you separate? Listen to silence: is it really silent? In *The Phantom Tollbooth* Milo discovers the Soundkeeper listening to a soundless radio:

"Isn't that lovely?" she sighed. "It's my favorite program — fifteen minutes of silence — and after that there's a half hour of quiet and then an interlude of lull. Why, did you know that there are almost as many kinds of stillness as there are sounds? . . . Have you ever heard the wonderful silence just before the dawn?" she inquired. "Or the quiet and calm just as a storm ends? Or perhaps you know the silence when you haven't the answer to a question you've been asked, or the hush in a country road at night, or the expectant pause in a roomful of people when someone is just about to speak, or, most beautiful of all, the moment after the door closes and you're all alone in the whole house? Each one is different, you know, and all very beautiful, if you listen carefully."

The Phantom Tollbooth also contains KAKOFONOUS A. DISCHORD, DOCTOR OF DISSONANCE — the A. stands for AS LOUD AS POSSIBLE — and his assistant, the awful DYNNE. Milo soon realizes that intense and prolonged noise can deafen him and you, just as you'll be blinded by staring at the sun or an arc welding lamp, or, less serious, you'll be unable to discriminate among other tastes if you cover everything with mustard. I read about a doctor who noticed that his daughter wasn't hearing him as he drove her home from a dance. He tested her and her friends and found that the amplified volume of the rock music was causing deafening.

What happens is that loud and continuous noise damages irreparably the microscopic hair cells that transmit sound from the ear to the brain. People in textile mills often suffer hearing loss, and airport workers must wear special earmuffs. When we say a noise is "deafening," it may really be just that. So if you value your ears, be careful how you expose them to the loud and the long. The whole volume of our culture has shot up, and "noise pollution" is now part of our vocabularies.

While you're consciously listening, make a list of all the sounds you can hear. When Demi was baby-sitting one night she wrote in her journal, "Rain on roof . . . dog breathing . . . drip of rain outside window . . . faint humming (refrigerator?) . . . Molly tossing in bed . . . creak of chair under me . . . sound of pen . . . clinking — ah, wind chimes on porch; two different tones — wonder when wind sprang up?"

These are quite refined "hears," almost as sensitive as Too-Too the owl in *Doctor Dolittle*, who listened at a closet door:

> "Sh! — Listen! — I do believe there's someone in there!"
> They all kept still a moment. Then the Doctor said:
> "You must be mistaken, Too-Too. I don't hear anything."
> "I'm sure of it," said the owl. "Sh! — there it is again —
> don't you hear that? . . . I hear the noise of some one putting his hand in his pocket." . . .

"But that makes hardly any sound at all," said the Doctor. "You couldn't hear that out here."

"Pardon me, but I can," said Too-Too. . . . "Almost everything makes *some* noise — if your ears are only sharp enough to catch it. Bats can hear a mole walking in his tunnel under the earth — and they think they're good hearers. But we owls can tell you, using only one ear, the colour of a kitten from the way it winks in the dark."

"Well, well!" said the Doctor. "You surprise me. That's very interesting. . . . Listen again and tell me what he's doing now." . . .

Too-Too leaned down and listened again very hard and long. At last he looked up into the Doctor's face and said:

"The man in there is unhappy. He weeps. He has taken care not to blubber or sniffle, lest we should find out that he is crying. But I heard — quite distinctly — the sound of a tear falling on his sleeve."

"How do you know it wasn't a drop of water falling off the ceiling on him?" asked Gub-Gub.

"Pshaw! — such ignorance!" sniffed Too-Too. "A drop of water falling off the ceiling would have made ten times as much noise!"

Other books will also help you to be more aware of sounds. *The Wind in the Willows,* especially "The Piper at the Gates of Dawn" chapter, and *Charlotte's Web,* and *Harriet* are stories that are listening all the time. In *The Animal Family* Randall Jarrell the poet gives bits like this:

The song ended on a long low note, and then everything was silent except the sea, whose shallow silver waves made a little hushing sound, and were silent for an instant, and then said *Hush!* again.

And William Mayne, in his *A Swarm in May,* describes organ music in myriad delightful ways, of which these are only a sample:

Dr. Sunderland was playing something that might have been "Boys and girls come out to play" again, leading them this time over stepping stones; with people falling into the stream occasionally. When they did, the shutters among the pipes hidden in the triforium above the choir would open suddenly to let out a surging splash of violins and flutes.

After Service Dr. Sunderland played music that was like a tangle of string: he pulled it through itself until he came to a knot; and there he had to wait and unpick, then pull and go on again. Then at last he was through. He wound the unknotted tune round his finger and thumb, tied it in a hank and he had finished.

Libby's introduction to the lumber camp, in *The Taste of Spruce Gum*, was through her ears: she awakened to the sound of the sawmill; and in *The Ghost Boat*, I had fun having Marcy follow a whole sequence in the dark:

Marcy listened to Thad's progress — a cracking twig, a stumbled footfall, a small splosh of water, a vexed mutter. She heard the dock creak, and then the large splash that meant Phil and his brother fish were safely back in the briny deep. Nearby she heard the rhythmic squeak and dip of the oars of some night rower. Then there was a sharp exclamation, the clatter of the bucket on the dock followed by a splat, and Thad's feet pounding back up the path.

In another spot she's telling a story about a swimmer:

"And she liked swimming underwater, too, because that didn't make any ripples at all, just bubbles — and she liked to listen to the bubbles come out of her nose and go up to the surface; they sounded just like the sound a bamboo wind-chime makes when the wind blows, all mingled and wooden and round. And she liked to take two stones and hit them together underwater, the clack-clack always sounded so faraway and mysterious, yet at the same time hurt her ears —"

I spent considerable time underwater, trying to figure out just what bubbles did sound like, and asking other people to submerge and listen, too.

There are other listening games. In nursery school Elspeth had a teacher who expanded the children's ears by making sounds for them to hear and identify. They'd all shut their eyes as she dropped an object on the floor, such as a pencil. Next she'd drop a block, and if you try it you'll notice there's quite a difference in sound between a dropped wooden block and a dropped wooden pencil. Or between a solid block and a hollow one. Those little kids got so they could tell by the chink whether it was a penny, nickel, dime, or quarter hitting the floor — very delicate nuances of sound. Can you tell the members of your family by their footsteps?

Pretend you've just been equipped with ears for the first time. What does the world sound like? What do you hear first? I've seen it happen in classes for the hard of hearing; the look on the face of a child who has just gotten his first hearing aid. My grandfather went deaf in his thirties, and knew he was going deaf. As a child I took his deafness for granted, learned the hand language, and often was chosen to go along with him to meetings or on trips. "Come be my ears," he would say, and I'd write down what was going on, on a long yellow tablet of lined paper. He died before I knew that I wanted to ask him a thousand things — about his life as a little boy, his feelings, especially about his deafness and his thoughts as he was going deaf. You could try pretending you're my grandfather, or that you've got "Three Days to Hear." What sounds will you store up in your mind's ear to last you a lifetime? Will you go to different places to hear certain sounds you don't want to miss?

Or pretend you're an animal, listening. What sounds does a cat select for cat-interest or self-preservation? What sounds does a deer? Or a turtle?

You might try a deafness game similar to the blindness one of blocking out the sense completely. It's harder, though, to cut out all sound than all light; loud noises get through. But I've seen study-muffs at college book stores that look like airport workers' muffs. I mean to buy a pair sometime, and really experience what my hearing means to me, once I don't have it.

All these ear-widenings you'll be writing down. Try lists, like Demi's. What you hear, also how you feel about it. My own lists of likes would include wind rattling a dry corn field; the squeaks and whuffs of a dog having a dream; water sounds in all their forms. I once asked Jill, when she was eight, what she liked best to hear, and she replied after a moment's reflection, "Waves on the shore and dogs far away barking." Elspeth, at four, said: "Leaves fluttering; the pages of books flapping, fli, fli, fli, like in the car when the window's open and a book's up behind." Megan's dislikes begin with the high-pitched snarl of a mosquito, and continue to chalk on a blackboard, fingernail on car finish, and Jill grinding her teeth in her sleep. There are raw materials for poems.

In describing sounds there's a special fun that you don't encounter in describing the other senses. When you describe a sight, for instance, the words you use can be vivid but won't *look* like that sight. Or in a taste description, the word doesn't produce the taste except in the imagination. But a word, since it is a *sound*, can often imitate pretty well the sound you want to describe. Elspeth did this unconsciously in "fli fli fli," also in "flap" and "flutter." Jarrell did it in "hush . . . hush" for slow waves. We all do it in words like gong, swish, hiss, pop, plop, splatter. This making words sound like what they're describing is called onomatopoeia. But when you're writing, try for the exact word, onomatopoetic or otherwise, that describes a sound. Tolly thinks of many words and comparisons for the wind. In "The Ballad of the Harp-Weaver" Edna St. Vincent Millay says, "A wind with a wolf's head howled about our door." And Robert Frost, in "Stopping by Woods on a Snowy Evening, ". . . The only other sound's the sweep / Of easy wind and downy flake." If you've ever heard that sort of winter wind, it actually is full of slow *e*'s, so that both the sound of it and the slow- ness are reproduced: "sweep" and "easy" are words it takes your tongue a while to pronounce. Try them out loud and see.

Deliberately reproducing the rhythm of a sound as well as the sound itself is also fun for a writer. You might not have caught it in "sweep of easy wind" since that rhythm is such a slow, wide-circling one, but how about here, in Frances Cornford's "The Watch"? There are sharp little words imitating the sharp little sound, but there is also the imitation of the rhythm:

> *I wakened on my hot, hard bed,*
> *Upon the pillow lay my head;*
> *Beneath the pillow I could hear*
> *My little watch was ticking clear.*
> *I thought the throbbing of it went*
> *Like my continual discontent,*
> *I thought it said in every tick:*
> *I am so sick, so sick, so sick;*
> *O death, come quick, come quick, come quick.*
> *Come quick, come quick, come quick, come quick.*

Robert Louis Stevenson often imitates actual rhythm in *A Child's Garden of Verses*. "How do you like to go up in a swing?" is a swinging rhythm; "Windy Nights" com- pares the wind to a galloping horse and uses a galloping rhythm:

> . . . *Late in the night when the fires are out,*
> *Why does he gallop and gallop about?*

Milne's poem really hops when Christopher Robin goes hoppity, hoppity, hoppity, hoppity hop, and Tennyson starts a poem,

> *Break, break, break*
> *On thy cold gray stones, O Sea!*

Not only can you imitate the actual sound and rhythm of something with words but you can also give the feel of a situation: slidey, sinuous sounds for smooth situations, harsh, grating sounds for brutal ones, sharp, nervous, fretful sounds for a situation like "The Watch."

So listen, and write. Try poems of what your ears hear. Tell stories, too, of times when sound made a difference to you, when you were aware of hearing or not hearing. For you are the only one who can hear what your ears hear. If you write down what you hear, we're all going to be richer. Not only will we hear what our own ears hear, but what yours do, too.

This will help our ears to hear even more, the next time.

6

I Didn't Mean to Be Bad

Marcy zipped the case around her cello, tucked her music in the back pocket, and sheathed her bow in the long pocket on the front. Behind her, Miss Fritz had already begun Sue Ellen's lesson. Sue Ellen was laboring through three octaves of E minor scales.

Marcy slung her cello against her side and tiptoed to the door. She opened it gently, stepped into the hall, and gave the door a good hard swing. The second before it slammed, she realized what she had done and stood paralyzed, while the whole building shuddered.

Sue Ellen stopped on a high D sharp. Miss Fritz's heels hit the floor and hurried across the room. The door was flung open but Marcy couldn't make herself turn.

"You didn't need to slam it," Miss Fritz said acidly, then all but slammed it herself, and returned to Sue Ellen. E minor started up again.

Marcy stood. She knew why she'd slammed the door. For the moment, going through the door frame, her mind vacant of thoughts, she'd had the sensation she was leaving her parents' bedroom, where the door never latched unless you gave it a vigorous swing. How many times she'd obeyed the command, "You have to *slam* that door!" This time she'd done it automatically, but how could she ever explain this to Miss Fritz? It was preposterous, unexplainable! Even if she could bring herself to try to tell her, Miss Fritz would never, never understand!

— From a book I'm someday going to write

THERE ARE PLENTY OF SITUATIONS where we really *do* mean to be bad. Where we are feeling so mean and horrid and ugly that we want to hurt somebody or something, and then we do. But let's think about those times in another chapter. Here let's talk about times when you (and I) behaved in all innocence, when your feelings were friendly, happy, joyful, curious, serene — and then *after* you'd done something, you discovered to your grief that whatever it was, wasn't acceptable. Your parents, or your music teacher, or your best friend were pretty angry and upset with you, maybe even thought you'd done it on purpose to be mean.

And so the pain of these situations is of a peculiar sort. When you've done something deliberately bad, you know there will likely be some sort of retribution — if you get caught — but when you do something with an innocent spirit, and retribution comes, the feelings you experience are especially poignant and unhappy. You hadn't been aware that others would take it this way, or that it would turn out as it did. This is particularly true when you're a small child because you haven't yet learned all the things that older people frown on, that the world frowns on. (Do we ever?) You tramp through wet cement as unconcernedly as a dog.

The farm I lived on as a child was also the home of my grandparents. Their house was almost as familiar to me as my own. I must have been three or four years old when I wandered one day into my grandmother's bedroom. There was her dressing table with its array of nail files, soft chamois buffers, powder boxes, lotion jars, combs, hairnets, and other things. I slid up on the stool and examined the fascinating items one by one. The one that held me most spellbound was a delicate pair of miniature scissors; I suppose they were cuticle scissors. I remember picking up those little, shiny, silver scissors. They fitted my thumb and fingers perfectly.

I snipped in the air with these for a few moments and then, naturally enough, looked around for something to cut. When a thing has a function, you want to exercise it. Alas for my grandma that there wasn't a newspaper lying on her bed! I noticed her closet door open a crack, climbed off the stool, and went in. I can still recall the feel of the limp dresses hanging around my ears. They had the special odor of my grandmother clinging to them, a little stale, a little perfumey. There were a few cotton house dresses, but this was her closet for her best dresses, the silks and chambrays that she wore to church. Down the line of my grandmother's dresses I went, and with that little scissors I snipped a small hole in each one. They cut beautifully. Satisfied, I returned them to the dressing table and wandered off in search of other entertainments.

It doesn't take much imagination to picture the next scene. That afternoon, or the next day, or the next Sunday, Grandma coming and slipping on a good dress, discovering a hole in it, her clack of dismay, taking it off, trying another one, discovering another hole, her greater dismay and bewilderment, her sudden suspicion, checking all the dresses, finding all the holes, and just at Jackie level. I don't remember what happened when the trail ended at me, or even whether I was punished. My mother thinks not, I was so small. But what stands out to me vividly, and why I remember this episode in such detail, was the shock of my discovery that I'd done something naughty, something that upset the grown-ups.

Other feelings certainly went along with this. I'm sure that once it was pointed out to me that dresses cost money and holes ruin dresses I realized it was a stupid thing to do. And even at three or four one feels chagrined to be stupid. I think also that normally nobody likes to inflict pain on other people, especially people one loves, and I must have felt unhappy that I was causing pain. There were probably also defensive feelings — I didn't know that I was doing something bad! And confused feelings. And a loss of self-respect. But these are all supposings. The only feeling I absolutely remember is total, astonishing surprise.

A boy once described to me a similar incident. Larry was about seven at the time and had been helping with the gardening. He had a great fondness for the green pepper bushes. If you've ever seen a green pepper growing, you'll know it grows on a little shrub. The leaves are glossy, and the green peppers are, too, hiding among the leaves; it's a very handsome plant. One day Larry decided he'd assist his father even more than required — without being asked. He got a bushel basket, went down the pepper rows, and picked every green pepper.

I've picked peppers, too, and know that they are very nice to pick. They come off with a satisfying snap, no twisting of the stem or anything, they feel plump and warm and polished in your hand, with sometimes an interesting convolution; in addition there's the setting — the smell of earth and greenery, the peaceful heat of the sun. The peppers, large and small, all look ripe (and are) so you don't have to make decisions. Larry told me he picked those green peppers with intense pleasure — three pleasures: the experience itself; the virtuous feeling that he was being a helpful boy; and the anticipation of his father's pleasure and praise. Well, his father wasn't pleased at all, and gave Larry a real walloping. And Larry never forgot it.

You've probably got a tulip story. Everybody does. Tulips snap as neatly as green peppers, and the stories are variations of, "When I was five I went into our neighbor's garden, slipped my fingers under each tulip blossom and snapped it off." You didn't do it maliciously but you also didn't miss a single tulip.

A grade school teacher told me that when she was a child in second grade her desk was next to the radiator. One day she accidentally touched it with her orange crayon. It melted down the side of the silver radiator in quite a lovely drip — so lovely that Martha took her other crayons and tried them all out. She'd transformed the radiator into a fairy rainbow before her teacher discovered what she was doing and charged up, herself a rainbow of wrath. When the radiator was cold Martha had to chip off all the crayon. No one appreciated the beauty, which had been her only concern, or thought that she had been anything but deliberately naughty.

This whole subject has a twist to it. You can understand, if you're reasonable, that cutting dresses or harvesting peppers prematurely might be logically considered wrong, even though you didn't realize it at the time. But I can imagine a situation where clipping dresses might be desirable, and I've walked through a hillside of so many wild daisies that the hundred or so that I pulled the heads off didn't even make a dent in that white blanket.

The problem of knowing when the situation is okay and when it isn't is complicated. It's hard enough to tell when you're a grown-up but it's a thousand times more complicated when you're a child. In a household, suppose there's something you like to do that is fine with your mother, but bothers your father, or your big sister? Is it right or is it wrong? Or worse, that sometimes bothers your mother but sometimes doesn't?

And then there are all the issues that even after they are explained you can't see where they are wrong. So that the problem is, you've done something bad according to everybody, but you think, "Is it really so awful? What are they making such a fuss about, anyway?" This brings feelings of rage and injustice.

Sometimes these stories are pretty painful to write, particularly if they've just happened recently and you're still smarting. It was easy enough for Debbie, at eleven, to write grown-up humor about the time, at age three, she got into the medicine cabinet (and whose fault was *that*?) and dumped everything into the toilet. What a remarkable sight it was, especially when she pulled the handle and there swirling around in the pink Lavoris water were the lavender pills and triangular pills and Uncle Lester's blue-green and yellow pills, and they all disappeared with a comfortable glug-glug. Well, the result of that was twofold. She was punished, and she was rushed to the hospital to have her stomach pumped, for her parents didn't know whether to believe that she hadn't swallowed any.

But suppose it was just this morning that you did something stupid or were badly misunderstood? Something that made you look mean or thoughtless or selfish or dumb or spiteful, and you didn't intend it at all? It happens to all of us, and these close scenes are harder to write about. They are so embarrassing, or they hurt so.

Yet there is a certain comfort in the writing. Getting it all down in ugly detail has a way of making you feel better, as well as often producing some pretty good writing. You feel it so keenly. And you don't always have to tell it in the first person, you know. Be anonymous. Tell it as though it happened to someone else. Change the name. Change the sex, if that doesn't make a difference. A girl could have picked those peppers. In the bit about slamming the door at the cello lesson I used different names for the girl and the teacher, but that misery happened to me. This way I could be more objective and yet put in all my horror and dismay.

From whatever point of view you write it, the main thing that will make it real and interesting will be the details that will let the reader see, feel, and live the story with you. The limp dresses, the sun-warmed peppers. While someone is reading your stuff they *are* you, and so give them as many clues as possible. Then they can feel what you felt, and the shock of discovery is theirs, and the walloping, too. It might start them off on stories of their own. When Kerry, ten, heard my scissors story, she dashed off her own dressing-table experience:

My mom's vanity was very short she had all her perfumes
and jewlry and if you have seen or if you have a mothers
vanity you will agree that it is very tempting so I decided
to be a momy and I got jewelry and powder and perfum
and lotion the lotin felt cool and the perfume smelled so
grown up the jewelry felt nice against my neck then I saw
my mother's lavendar nighty on the floor and I put it on
then I ran down the hall it streamed out behind me and I
felt like a new butterfly just learning to fly but not flying
just skimming along the ground —

And then the tripping, the tearing, the reckoning. Kerry
hadn't meant to be bad, either.

7

Eavesdrop!

"And what is the use of a book," thought Alice, "without
pictures or conversations?"

— From *Alice's Adventures in Wonderland*,
by Lewis Carroll

I was talking with Jill's class, when she was in fifth
grade, about reading and writing, and discovered that most
of them choose a library book the way I usually do — and
as Alice did, and as you no doubt do, too. Don't you riffle
through the pages, look at the pictures, and see how much
conversation there is? And whether that conversation
catches you and leads you along like salted peanuts? If
a book presents page after page of long, unbroken paragraphs, we're not so likely to take it out and give it a try.
(And of course, we miss some good books that way.)

We went on to discuss the conversation, how in some books the speech is very stilted and unreal, and you think to yourself, "*Nobody* ever talks like this!" Whereas in other books it sounds absolutely natural, so genuine that it doesn't even occur to you to stop and think about the speech at all.

And we talked about Harriet. If she's not your personal friend, you're missing something. *Harriet the Spy*, by Louise Fitzhugh. It's out in paperback. Harriet's ten or so, and her ambition is to be a spy — and a writer. The two really go hand in hand. She carries a notebook and in it writes down the observations she makes on her spy route. She also records her thoughts, not only from the route, but from everywhere:

HE LOVES TO DO THAT. IS THIS WHAT OLE GOLLY MEANS? SHE SAYS PEOPLE WHO LOVE THEIR WORK LOVE LIFE. DO SOME PEOPLE HATE LIFE? ANYWAY I WOULDN'T MIND LIVING LIKE HARRISON WITHERS BECAUSE HE LOOKS HAPPY EXCEPT I WOULDN'T LIKE *ALL* THOSE CATS. I MIGHT EVEN LIKE A DOG.

ONCE I THOUGHT I WANTED TO BE FRANCA AND LIVE IN THAT FAMILY. BUT SHE'S SO DULL IF I WAS HER I COULDN'T STAND MYSELF. I GUESS IT'S NOT MONEY THAT MAKES PEOPLE DULL. THERE IS A LOT I DON'T KNOW ABOUT THIS THING OF BEING DULL. I BETTER FIND OUT BECAUSE I MIGHT BE IT.

WHY DON'T THEY SAY WHAT THEY FEEL? OLE GOLLY SAID "ALWAYS SAY EXACTLY WHAT YOU FEEL. PEOPLE ARE HURT MORE BY MISUNDER-STANDING THAN ANYTHING ELSE." AM I HURT? I DON'T FEEL HURT. I JUST FEEL FUNNY ALL OVER.

She watches people but she also listens. She listens in alleys, at windows, through skylights, in dumbwaiters, at the top of stairs, through cracks in doors. She is a master eavesdropper, which is a marvelous word that means listening, unseen, at the eaves of a house. And she writes down what she hears, to think about.

I was recommending to Jill's friends that they make a habit of carrying "Harriet notebooks," or record books, which I talk about in the "Me Best Thoughts" chapter. And also, that they become listeners. But I was a little worried that they'd go home and tell their parents that Jill's mother had urged them to eavesdrop, to be sneaky, and some irate parent would call up the teacher or principal, who, heaven knows, had enough irate parents to deal with. So I started to tell them ways of listening *without* being a sneak, or without *quite* being one (there's a fine edge, you know), but they didn't want to hear that: they all wanted to tell me, and each other, how skillful they already were at dropping at the eaves. I found out there wasn't a thing I, or Harriet, could teach them. Dark stair tops? Which creaky step to look out for? Big sisters' telephone conversations? Cracks of doors? Tree limbs? That hidey space behind the couch? They knew them all.

They also fully agreed that listening involved danger. Two sorts. Sometimes you're caught, and then you get it. Sometimes — and this is worse — you hear things you wish you hadn't, and you know you shouldn't. You might realize, from a snatch of conversation, that you don't have all the pieces of the jigsaw puzzle, you misunderstand, you may draw false conclusions as well as unhappy true ones. But since you're eavesdropping, it's very hard to go to the person and admit you've listened, and get the story straight. You may hurt yourself inside, without anyone discovering that you've eavesdropped. It can also happen in all innocence. Demi once crawled into a dark closet to nurse a wounded spirit, at a house where we were visiting, and overheard a conversation in the next room that was definitely not intended for her ears.

But there *are* ways of listening that aren't quite so sneaky as others, and these I'd like to share with you, if you haven't discovered them already for yourself. The secret is simple: *You can listen to an awful lot if people don't think you're listening!*

It's amazing what they'll say in front of you. For most people — teachers and parents are no exceptions — have the fixed idea that you have to be looking at what you're listening to, or you aren't paying attention. If your blue eyes are fastened on the speaker, then you're listening. If they're not, you're not. Both statements may be completely untrue but that doesn't matter so long as people believe them.

So, how do we put this nugget to use?

I eavesdropped on a fascinating conversation in a dime store once. Two little girls were there with their mothers; the mothers were talking and pushing carts while the little girls — about four and five years old — were also engaged in a conversation. I pricked up my ears when the older of the girls cried out, "But you *do* like me, you *do* like me!"

"I don't," said the other one, softly.

The older girl, more agitated, wailed, "But you *have* to like me, I'm your *friend*, I'm *nice*, you *do* like me!"

"I don't."

The older girl, almost in tears, pulled on her mother's coat. "Mother! She says she doesn't like me! She doesn't like me!" The mother, absorbed with her friend, just brushed the child off and the girl wept again to her companion, "You *do* like me! I know you do!"

"No, I don't."

I followed that little scene all the way around the five-and-dime, watching the callousness of the mothers, seeing the older girl become more and more frantic and the younger one more and more smug as she saw what power to devastate she held in her words.

Rereading this I see I've used "eye" terms: watch, see. Actually I was only taking an occasional furtive glance. What I *was* doing was flapping my ears while examining everything in the dime store. Fingering stuff off the counters, and staying close to this unhappy drama.

This technique works in stores. In houses, buses, subways, waiting rooms, on rocks, or fallen logs, or grass, what you do is bury yourself in reading matter or (not quite so good) sit or lie with closed eyes. The speakers will think you're concentrating on the print and don't hear, or else that you're asleep. They'll look at you, maybe, and lower their voices, but if you don't show any flicker of interest they'll go on talking. You mustn't forget to turn a page occasionally, though. Or take a deep breath and shift your position.

One might ask, why does it matter whether we're any type of listener at all? Wild sneaks, garden-variety sneaks, half-sneaks, or hybrid? Heather, who's thirteen now, could give a main reason. When she was in fourth grade she came home from school one noon and blurted to her mother, "I like my teacher so much and she's so interesting, and I was just standing there listening to her talk to a lady and she looked at me and she said, 'Heather, you know it's not polite to listen in on other people's conversation.' I went away and cried. It was just because I thought she was so *interesting*."

I cry with you, Heather. I find people so interesting, too, and I can't listen in on a fraction of what I'd like to, because it isn't polite. If you'd been less open and honest, if you'd pretended to read a book or do a lesson, you might have listened in without a reprimand.

On a date once I visited an amusement pier at Lake Geneva; it was almost like a carnival or penny arcade, and one of the booths held a small ferretlike man, a handwriting analyzer, or graphologist: learn your personality through your handwriting. So for fun and fifty cents I gave him a sample of my scrawl. He studied it, and proceeded to tell me all sorts of things about myself as revealed through the way I dotted my *i*'s, completed my *s*'s, slanted my letters, and so forth. I don't recall the bulk of his description, but toward the end he said, "You are very curious." He hesitated, then looked up at me with a quick flash in his shrewd, narrowed eyes, and a little quirk of a smile. "You're more than curious. You're *nosy*."

Well, he had my number, all right. I like to know things, to find out how things work and why, how ants and animals behave, especially how we people think and have behaved, from the time we painted cave walls up till now. I find it all terribly interesting, like Heather and Harriet, so interesting (and moving and important) that I don't want to keep it to myself but to share it the best I can.

The best way I've found so far, not counting having a family, is by writing stories. I have a high regard for stories, because so many of the realest meanings about things have hit me through great stories: *The Secret Garden*, *Wind in the Willows*, *A Boy of the Lost Crusade*, *At the Back of the North Wind*, *The Princess and Curdie*, *Alice*, *The Bluebird*, stories I read over and over when I was little; books like *The Animal Family* and the *Hobbit* and Narnia sagas, which I've only read since being grown. These sorts of books tell you much more about the Great Mysteries than a book like this one, because while reading them you *are* Mary and Colin and Diamond and Curdie and Mole and Tyltyl and they remain part of you forever — for you get gripped in the heart, where it lasts, rather than just reading my telling you that I got gripped in the heart.

But to circle back then to conversations. When someone tells me something that's happened to him, I love him to report the exact conversation, the *he sez's* and *she sez's*. "What did you say next?" I ask, and "What did he say then?"

I like the same thing in reading a book. I don't want

some writer to *tell* me that Colin staged a tantrum and so Mary staged a countertantrum; I want to hear the tantrums myself. It's more fun because it's more direct, firsthand instead of second. This allows me to interpret the situation for myself. It's more demanding of my brain cells.

I like to do this in my own writing, too, to see how much I can put across in the conversation without *telling* the reader anything at all. I can plant clues, carry the story forward, through the speech. This is more challenging to write, more fun, and more the way life really is. For usually there isn't somebody standing by like a Greek chorus, interpreting things for us as we trudge along.

I also like to be sparing about the adverbs that tell you *how* a thing is said. If your words are angry enough, or the situation whispery enough, you shouldn't have to say "she said angrily," or "he said softly." Usually on my first draft they all go in, and in the rewrites three-quarters of them get pitched out. There's an old series of books that overuses those conversational adverbs so dreadfully, the *Tom Swift* books, that a game arose a while ago in the *Saturday Review* magazine called Tom Swifties. You try to think up a sentence where the words spoken make a pun with the adverb. "I ripped my new wool coat," she said sheepishly, or, "I'm going to find that hound if it's the last thing I do," he said doggedly. The best one I ever made up was, "You'll *never* get me to take a bite of that apple," he said adamantly.

But to write genuine conversations takes listening, not just to TV or radio or movie scripts, or to the dialogues you're a part of — for then they're partly in your own image — but to all sorts of people using all sorts of words in all sorts of ways: eating, arguing, loving, fretting, kidding, swearing, lecturing, everything. If you do this you'll discover that people, as I said in the "Woodies" chapter, talk very differently. Some are monotones, not only in their tones, but in their words, their ideas — same dull thoughts, dreary clichés. Some may seem dry as dust but as you listen you find a vein of humor flowing under the surface. Or, as in the book *Mary Poppins*, a tart tongue may hide love.

When I wrote *The Taste of Spruce Gum* I had a wonderful source of raw material — Grandma Vi Tuttle, then in her eighties. I took down her words about life on Shrewsbury Mountain as she spoke them, and when I got writing the story, making up the conversation, I used as many of her expressions as I could: "Tough as tripe," "I wouldn't trust him any further'n I could throw a cat by the tail," "I didn't know him from a fence post." The part about her courtship in chapter one is almost word for word as she told it to me, and so is the vivid description of the railroad accident where Mr. Reed and Mrs. Vincent were killed but her husband was saved. Vi, who just died in her midnineties, graduated from a rural Illinois high school around 1900, taught school in Illinois for several years before her marriage and also on the mountain in Vermont after it. She was an intelligent woman, a reader of more than bookclub condensations up to her death, alert and active all her life, yet she spoke a kind of colloquial English with mistakes of pronunciation and grammar that I found very refreshing. I used her speech as the model for all the speech in the book — the rock on which I anchored my imagination.

But a copy editor, whose job it is in a publishing company to read manuscripts and set wrongs right, took exception to the speech in the book, and she changed all my (Grandma Vi's) words to standard English. Schoolmarm English. Also a lot of the punctuation, which I was using to imitate the rhythm and music of spoken words.

I glumly reviewed the manuscript when it came back to me, heaved various sighs, and in a depressed state finally called together my husband and our good friends Jake and Mary, who are readers, poets, and scholars, and sensitive to words and people. I wanted to know if I was being picky or unreasonable to be unhappy about a comma removed here, a "he don't" changed to "he doesn't" there. We slogged through the manuscript for a ways and all of a sudden Jake banged his fist down on the card table and snarled, "They're trying to get you to write *homogenized* English!"

So I changed everything back to the way it had been and wrote a three-page defense to my editor which said in essence: "I want readers to say, not 'How unlikely that Mama, an educated woman and schoolteacher, would talk that way,' but 'So *that's* how a woman with a rural Illinois high school education at the turn of the century talked!' " My editor said, "All right, we'll let it stand, we'll see what the reviewers think." The reviewers, when the book came out, commented on the naturalness of the speech. Grandma Vi's speech. I'll save more stories on Grandma Vi, and the tracking down of "fills," a word mystery I'd never have encountered without listening, for later.

So *listening* can be your antidote to homogenizing your language. In the "Awakened Eye" chapter, I said I wrote mainly by eye. I see now that's much too narrow. The moving picture that goes on in my head has a sound track and I hear what's going on, too — and write down the conversation the way it's being spoken.

When I was writing *Missing Melinda* I was teaching children's literature at one of Kent State's extension centers, and had to drive an hour there and back on the thruway, two nights a week. I wrote a lot of the book in my head on those trips, muttering it to myself. I had two "accidents." Once I got so engrossed in my imagination that I passed the Kent exit and had to drive forty miles farther to the Warren one — eighty miles extra, at eleven o'clock at night, with a screaming baby waiting up at home to be nursed. The other time a policeman stopped me to see whether I was drunk. I only then realized I was punctuating my "mind conversations" with the gas pedal — speeding up at the exciting places, slowing down suddenly, making little erratic spurts. I convinced him I was okay and drove on soberly, trying not to think about anything but the road, which makes driving a bore, but safer.

A final reason for listening, beyond mere interest and good writing: Almost everybody talks, hardly anybody listens. Really listens. Jesus said, "They have ears but hear not," and he meant, as in his similar reference to eyes, perceiving with the heart. A slave boy in *Treasure of Green Knowe* says to blind Susan, "You blind, but you see things sometimes when I can't." He could have added, "You hear things, too":

> All these talkers behaved freely, as though Susan, because she couldn't see them, couldn't hear them either, or at least did not count. But Susan heard far more than other people and understood it better too. She had nothing to do but listen — hers was a world of voices. Voices did not deceive her, and she could not see the smiles that were meant to deceive. She knew at once what people really meant, what they thought of the person they were speaking to, and even what they didn't say.

What they didn't say. What they meant to say. What's between the words, and behind them, and underneath them. What they want you to hear, but don't know how to say, and might not be able to, even if they knew how.

That's listening with the heart. And if you can do that, even if you can never write a sentence, you're worth more than ten thousand who can.

8

Will You, Won't You Join the Dance?

Y OU'RE PROBABLY NOT WONDERING MUCH why I've called
this book *Turn Not Pale, Beloved Snail.* But maybe you
are a little, since titles are parts of books. Anyway, I
want to tell you. But you'll need to read first my second-
favorite poem by Lewis Carroll (my first-favorite is "The
Walrus and the Carpenter"). It's sung by the Mock Turtle
in *Alice's Adventures in Wonderland,* while he and the
Gryphon solemnly dance the "Lobster-Quadrille":

"Will you walk a little faster?" said a whiting to a snail,

"There's a porpoise close behind us, and he's treading on
    my tail.
See how eagerly the lobsters and the turtles all advance!
They are waiting on the shingle — will you come and join
    the dance?

Will you, won't you, will you, won't you, will you join the
    dance?
Will you, won't you, will you, won't you, won't you join
    the dance?

"You can really have no notion how delightful it will be
When they take us up and throw us, with the lobsters, out
    to sea!"
But the snail replied "Too far, too far!" and gave a look
    askance —
Said he thanked the whiting kindly, but he would not join
    the dance.

Would not, could not, would not, could not, would not join
    the dance.
Would not, could not, would not, could not, could not join
    the dance.

"What matters it how far we go?" his scaly friend replied,
"There is another shore, you know, upon the other side.
The further off from England the nearer is to France —
Then turn not pale, beloved snail, but come and join the
    dance.

Will you, won't you, will you, won't you, will you join the
    dance?
Will you, won't you, will you, won't you, won't you join
    the dance?

A lot of times people think writers are only observers
of life. Watchers of the dance. They sit apart and look on,

73

and they write it all down in their books, what the steps are, how well or badly everybody else is doing the steps, and then others can read the books and find out what life, what the dance, is all about.

Some writers believe this, too. Maybe they really think this is the best way to write — how can you be scribbling about the dance while you're dancing it? It's tricky, of course. See Demi's comments on this very problem in the "Me Best Thoughts" chapter. I'm all for watching, but I'm even more for dancing, and I think the proper sort of watching is a part of the dance. While you're dancing you're also listening, looking, feeling, and so forth, and storing up all these things inside yourself. So that when you stop for breath, or when the dance slows down a little, you are able to jot it down. For me, the actual writing is part of the dance, and makes the dance even better.

I think it's more that people are afraid. They're really scared of the dance underneath — maybe that they won't dance well enough? They'll look silly? They might be bored? Somebody will tread on their tail — and so they sit off on the sidelines and look, and their excuse is that they're studying it, or writing about it, so they can't participate.

But really, to understand the dance, you have to be in it — up to your neck. (You see I'm continuing Lewis Carroll's watery images!) Then you're not supposing other people's feelings about the dance. You know your own, and those are a springboard to how others feel. Your writing will be more genuine. Sitting off, what you mainly learn is how it feels *not* to join the dance.

So the title of this book is urging you not to be afraid to try new things, which include writing, but that's only a little part of it. Don't hang back. Don't say I can't swim, or I'm afraid, or that doesn't look like fun, or I'd rather watch it on TV, or I'll get my feet wet, or so-and-so tried that once and didn't like it. Everything you participate in becomes part of you. Walter de la Mare says it in the poem, "Miss T.," using food for his image, instead of the dance:

> It's a very odd thing —
> As odd as can be —
> That whatever Miss T. eats
> Turns into Miss T; . . .

Everything that's part of you can be part of your writing. If your innards are rich and interesting, your writing is apt to be, too. Alfred, Lord Tennyson (the long silky beard on the Authors cards. Does anybody play Authors anymore? We used to call his *Idyls of the King* "Piddles of the King" and laugh uproariously) — anyway, he says it in another way in *Ulysses*:

> . . . I am a part of all that I have met;
> Yet all experience is an arch wherethrough
> Gleams that untravell'd world, whose margin fades
> Forever and forever when I move. . . .

In other words, the dance leads on to more dance. You have to take the first step, and then keep moving. You'll leave England, where you feel safe, but

> "What matters it how far we go?" his scaly friend replied,
> "There is another shore, you know, upon the other side.
> The further off from England the nearer is to France —
> Then turn not pale, beloved snail, but come and join the
>   dance."

That's all.

SOME EXAMPLES OF THE DANCE

When I was little I took violin lessons. Every spring there'd be a recital. I can remember standing in the hallway, my fiddle under my arm, trying to rub the cold sweat off the palms of my hands onto my satin dress. I both wanted to play and dreaded it. Then came the terrible, wonderful moment when it was my turn, and legs not my own marched me out in front of the piano, and there in the dimness of the audience sat the family, with my little brother smirking and making faces. I tucked my fiddle under my chin, the piano struck the opening chords, I started out on the first tremulous tones with wavering bow and in my stomach strong waves of almost nausea . . . then gradually came the confidence: it's going all right, I'm going to make it, my bow has quit bouncing! — and the forgetting of the lights and audience, and finally the exhilaration of coming through and knowing I'd done a passable job, maybe even a good one in spite of a few mistakes. And the blessed relief of having it over.

I understand stage fright from the inside. I can believe it when Pablo Casals, in his nineties and the world's greatest cellist, said he still had stage fright when he performed.

Another time I remember is when our family drove to Florida once. My father noticed fishing boats at a wharf in St. Petersburg. We stopped, and my father, always one to join the dance, got talking to a fisherman who had a cargo of fresh oysters. The first thing I knew, the man had pulled out his knife and was opening up raw oysters while my father was gulping them down with gusto. Then the oyster man began passing them out to all of us. I was appalled. They looked terrible, pearly gray and blobby, slimy, with curvy bits and unidentifiable parts, lying there in the shells in a murky soup of their own juices. I'd eaten oyster stew but it had never occurred to me that an oyster was anything to eat *raw*. Well, I took one and put it in my mouth, but there was something about its texture that prevented me from swallowing it. I eased it out into my hand and after a moment tried again, but again it wouldn't go down. That oyster went in and out several times as I gagged on swallowing it. Finally I dropped it into the water between the boat and the dock, feeling a little ashamed that I hadn't measured up.

A third story: joining the dance doesn't necessarily mean rah-rah doing what everyone else is doing. You can dance alone. Once in the Wisconsin north woods my whole family was going fishing, but I was tired of fishing. So I stayed onshore and wandered around in the woods. After a while I lay down and discovered under my nose some tiny plants in a patch of moss. They had little, gray-green, rough stems and were capped by tiny bright-red innertubes. They looked like something that might grow on Mars. I was fascinated, found more, got a pan to preserve some, and carried them home from our vacation. I took them to a biology teacher and found out they were *two* kinds of lichen: the green and the red, each necessary to the other to live. And I learned a new word, symbiosis, that describes this relationship.

In these three stories I could have refused the experiences: playing in the recital, trying the oyster, walking alone in the woods. One of the problems all of us have today is that mostly we don't even get the chance to choose. And this is especially bad for kids, for now is the time when you should be having hundreds and thousands of firsthand experiences, building up your experience-vocabulary. Collecting the grains of sand that cause the pearls to grow, the specks of dust that are necessary for a raindrop to form.

You should have the creative fun of making dolls and dressing them, rather than having Barbie and her wardrobe all designed for you; inventing and building toys rather than getting them all punched out of plastic where all you do is glue them together; painting your own pictures instead of painting by number.

One experience we all have that's so common it's hardly worth writing about is ripping open frozen peas and dumping them in boiling water. But how drab this is, compared to picking them: selecting the plump pods from the skinny on the tangled vines, and then sitting with a basin in your lap and learning just where to press your thumb in order to make the shell pop open, and running your thumb down the row of peas as they sit there so self-satisfied. "Like so many peas in a pod" becomes a cliché with meaning. The eating of fresh peas instead of frozen is vastly different, too! Opening frozen strawberries is much the same experience as opening frozen peas, but the picking of the two is very different. There is more temptation to eat strawberries as you pick, the plants are different, the feel of a strawberry is quite unlike that of a pea pod. And hulling a strawberry is a separate skill. But for most of us, picking peas and strawberries are experiences that we have to go out and hunt for. They don't fall in our laps.

What does fall is that most popular of spectator sports, the secondhand canned experience of TV. There the world parades before us in a little box and we shift the gears of our emotions every fifteen minutes, so that grief, and fear, and even laughter become cheap because we're using them so rapidly on unreal, quickly forgotten stuff. Sure, we learn a lot from TV. There are even some worthwhile programs. But I maintain that one ride on a horse will stick with you longer than a thousand TV westerns.

Thinking about horses: I refused to join the dance, in a

sense, with a horse that we got on the farm when I was about twelve. I was afraid to let him go fast for fear of getting hurt, so for months I held him down to a trot. You'll know, if you've ever been an amateur rider, that sticking on a trotting horse is like going over a washboard road filled with potholes in a jeep, it shakes the fillings out of you and gives you one heck of a sore bottom. Well, finally the horse got fed up and one day he just took the bit in his teeth — there's another cliché — and galloped. It was marvelous! It was like rocking in a lawn chair and flying at the same time. My first terror was replaced with exhilaration, and some self-disgust: all those months of needless suffering! Both for me and the horse.

Sometimes in joining the dance you *will* get hurt. A friend of ours, Francis, got Putzi for a birthday present when he was small and Putzi was a pup. He loved her with a deep, deep love. When he would lie on his stomach, reading, the plump dachshund would lie for hours on his legs with her chin resting on the mound of his rump. They were best friends. And then one day Putzi died. Francis said to me, "I've learned one thing — never to love anything that much. Then you won't get hurt." That was his immediate reaction, in his grief. Later he realized that the pain of not loving is a more serious hurt. Now he has another dog, and while Pip can never take Putzi's special place, Pip has her own special place and is well loved.

Have you stories like these to write about? Were you afraid to join the dance, and then did? Or refused, and were sorry? Joined and had "good" hurts? "Bad" hurts? It seems to me the only bad hurts are the ones that instead of opening you to further dancing, shut the door and close you up. It's an experience to jump in front of a truck, all right, but if you do it, you may never dance again.

Have you ever wanted to share your experiences with someone else? Robert Frost does, in "The Pasture":

I'm going out to clean the pasture spring;
I'll only stop to rake the leaves away
(And wait to watch the water clear, I may):
I shan't be gone long. — You come too.

I'm going out to fetch the little calf
That's standing by the mother. It's so young
It totters when she licks it with her tongue.
I shan't be gone long. You come too.

I could have used this poem instead of "The Lobster-Quadrille." It's also an invitation to the dance. He wants you to share the experiences that are meaningful to him — the spring, the calf — because he cares about you. The poem is an invitation to companionship — "I want a sympathetic human being along." You are his beloved snail.

So that's the last thing. If we're taking part in something, *really* dancing, then we're putting life and time and energy into it. We're loving Putzi, we're giving our hearts and souls. When we're doing this, we care. I don't know about you, but I can't write well about anything I don't care about. To me the writing is second to the caring, a way of communicating the caring. Hoping you'll care, that you'll come, too. And this caring is the heart of the dance, and is the most important thing in the world.

9

The Garlic Sang

> . . . he took care to include a yard of long French bread, a
> sausage out of which the garlic sang, some cheese which lay
> down and cried. . . .
>
> — From *The Wind in the Willows,*
> by Kenneth Grahame

THAT PASSAGE CELEBRATES TASTE, I think, though Rat and
Mole are savoring the food through their other senses, too
— something we all do, particularly with smell, whether
we are aware of it or not. For it's not easy to separate taste
from smell, as you realize when you have a cold. Food is
flat and tasteless when your nose is stuffy. Or perhaps
you've noticed that when you're very thirsty and glug
something down rapidly, a glass of lemonade, you don't
really taste the drink (after its first contact with your
tongue) until the final swallow and air floods back into

your nose and throat. Till then the lemonade might just as well be water. If you really want to savor a drink you take small sips, as with an after-dinner liqueur or brandy, and this allows your nose, with its experience, to enrich your tongue. For the tongue alone distinguishes only four broad tastes: sweet, sour, bitter, and salt; but coupled with smell our tongues have infinite discrimination.

You might have fun, as I did in a biology class, finding out where on your tongue these different tastes are, for though each taste bud picks up its own particular responsibility, the buds are not distributed randomly, but like-buds cluster together. In class we put something bitter on the end of a toothpick and touched all over our tongues till we'd found the total area that responded to "bitter" and then we marked it on a tongue map. We did the same for the other three tastes. I've found this knowledge a great help in taking nasty medicine. And talking about tongues: I don't suppose I need to recommend that you examine yours in a mirror. It's a fascinating study, especially the less noticed underside which reminds me of the innards of a clam, only more colorful.

Both in writing and actual living I feel the sense of taste is a poor cousin to the "more important" senses of sight and sound. You might argue that this is natural, since we don't *use* our tasting equipment nearly as much as our eyes and ears, unless our profession is tea-taster, wine-taster, or cheese-taster, and if one had to give up one of those three senses, there'd be no question which would lose out. Also, our eyes have to rest on *something*, unless they are closed or it is absolutely dark, and similarly our ears are rarely if ever in a situation of total silence. So we are constantly exposed to sight and sound, whereas our tongues for the most part rest quietly against the roofs of our mouths, and I've never noticed that my roof has any exotic or interesting taste. (What *does* spit taste like, anyway? Does it seem tasteless merely because we're so used to it?) Oh yes, we talk. But then our tongues are bathed in equally tasteless air.

Even though we don't use our taste sense as much as the others, I think its neglect goes deeper than this. Maybe it has to do with an old — and false — religious split between the mind, or spirit, and the body. It was better to be "of the spirit" than "of the flesh," and so the senses that smacked more of the body — touching, tasting, smelling — were considered more base than seeing and hearing, where there is at least a cushion of air between the ear and what's making the noise, or the eye and what it sees. But with noses we're getting uncomfortably close, and when we come to touch, our skin is actually in contact. But consider taste: if we're going to live we have to eat, and when you think about it, what a gross activity!

Here you pick up something, actually take your environment, and put it in that pink cavity and crack it and mash it all around with that odd looking flap of muscle, and swallow it down your gullet, and then various peculiar things happen to it. Megan the other day came back from school and asked, "Why do you have to have that *whole big liver* just to do *that?*" And she found it so distasteful — notice the word — that she didn't want to explain about the liver making bile which pours into the intestine at some point or other, and finishes the digestive process.

By the time we get down to the guts we're pretty basic. We know things are getting used up, and we've known since our own toilet training that we're not supposed to talk about these things, unless in a detached manner, using the acceptable words. All this is the end product of taking in, engorging (like an amoeba), tasting. And because of our distaste with waste products we've ignored them or flushed them away, and the world is now approaching a gigantic cesspool. We're discovering that we've got to talk about waste products, and at dinner, too. But that's another whole chapter — or book.

But back to the other end of the alimentary canal. If we enjoy our food, how marvelous! We should. And what a great gift from the universe or Whoever was our maker, that not only can we taste, but that there is such a tremendous variety of tastes for us to enjoy. Yet how many of us feel embarrassed, as if we're too earthy, too aware of our senses, if we eat with gusto? We can't burp, we can't slurp, we fence the whole process around with all sorts of manners. We mustn't eat like pigs.

I always loved to go alor.g to feed the pigs. It was such a pleasure to watch them come racing, ears flapping, squealing and crowding up to the fence, scrambling on top of each other in their eagerness, their stomachs the most important thing in the world, their only care. Billy Beadle would push through the mob and empty a can of milk slops into the trough, maybe right on the heads of a few, and the bedlam would be deafening as every pig tried to cram his snout in. And then all the gulps and schlurps as the food was drained. I suppose I enjoyed it vicariously — I knew I couldn't eat that way myself, or show my pleasure so heartily.

E. B. White rivals Kenneth Grahame in his huge enjoyment of food. He tells about it from several points of view, or should I say, tips-of-tongue? Here he describes Wilbur the pig's dinner, in *Charlotte's Web:*

> Wilbur stood in the trough, drooling with hunger. Lurvy poured. The slops ran creamily down around the pig's eyes and ears. Wilbur grunted. He gulped and sucked, and sucked and gulped, making swishing and swooshing noises, anxious to get everything at once. It was a delicious meal — skim milk, wheat middlings, leftover pancakes, half a doughnut, the rind of a summer squash, two pieces of stale toast, a third of a gingersnap, a fish tail, one orange

peel, several noodles from a noodle soup, the scum off a cup of cocoa, an ancient jelly roll, a strip of paper from the lining of the garbage pail, and a spoonful of raspberry jello.

Here are Charlotte's spidery tastes:

"You mean you *eat* flies?" gasped Wilbur.

"Certainly. Flies, bugs, grasshoppers, choice beetles, moths, butterflies, tasty cockroaches, gnats, midges, daddy longlegs, centipedes, mosquitoes, crickets — anything that is careless enough to get caught in my web. I have to live, don't I?"

"Why, yes, of course," said Wilbur. "Do they taste good?"

"Delicious. Of course, I don't really eat them. I drink them — drink their blood. I love blood," said Charlotte, and her pleasant, thin voice grew even thinner and more pleasant.

And how about that disgusting rat, Templeton, whose tastes run to the rotten egg under Wilbur's trough and the residue from old, discarded lunch boxes at the fair?

Kenneth Grahame's animals, on the other hand, are more nearly ourselves in fur. Toads, moles, water rats alike have a human palate:

He . . . reappeared staggering under a fat, wicker luncheon-basket. . . .

"What's inside it?" asked the Mole, wiggling with curiosity.

"There's cold chicken inside it," replied the Rat briefly; "coldtonguecoldhamcoldbeefpickledgherkinssaladfrenchrolls cresssandwidgespottedmeatgingerbeerlemonadesodawater —"

"O stop, stop," cried the Mole in ecstasies: "This is too much!"

"Do you really think so?" inquired the Rat seriously. "It's only what I always take on these little excursions. . . ."

How can we improve our "taste quotient" for richer living, spicier writing? The answer is obvious: go on tasting, and don't be satisfied with your own narrow taste vocabulary.

It's essential to be willing to try new things. At friends' houses, if they're in a different cooking rut from your house, you'll have a chance to sample different sorts of cookery. When we were little we once hiked across the field to another farm and the kids treated us to mustard and sugar sandwiches. Now *there's* a taste thrill. At restaurants you might order unusual dishes, or at least sample the baby eel and avocado salad your father ordered, even though it looks like a mess of angleworms on a bed of goat cud. You understand, too, that you have to be willing to try restaurants beyond Freddie's Hamburger Heaven.

Demi, Megan, and Jill are together in a French class at their school, and on the last day they prepared and ate a typical French meal. In a previous school Demi ate Russian style in her Russian class, and in her world lit class, the group prepared a dish native to each country whose literature they studied.

Try collecting unusual tastes. Sample all the various spices — alone and in food: ginger, curry, cumin. Try spruce gum. In my book *The Taste of Spruce Gum*, Libby first encounters that novel sensation:

> Mama was making faces. . . . "I can't see how he could like it! It's pure turpentine!" She turned and spit. Libby was startled. When had she seen Mama spit, in Illinois?
>
> "Here, Libby," chuckled Uncle Charles. "See if you're more a Vermonter than your ma." In his palm rested an amber lump. Bits of bark crusted it, and the edges were crumbled like dirty sugar. She took it gingerly, careful not to touch his hand, and chewed it.
>
> It shattered into a thousand pieces. Mama was right. It tasted all resiny. She wanted to spit, too — but Papa had

liked spruce gum. Uncle Charles twitched the reins and Old
Tom started. Now the gum began to wad, and the piney
taste was somewhat fresh and pleasant.

"Can you stand it?" marveled Mama.

"You have to get used to it," Libby said, and Uncle
Charles chuckled again.

I first encountered spruce gum in Vermont the summer
after we were married. Bob had gone to a camp in New
Hampshire when he was twelve and chewed it there, and
was now looking forward to making a collection of this
delicacy when a bunch of us climbed Camel's Hump. He
circled every spruce on the trail and examined it for the
delectable lumps, but after the first few finds there weren't
any more. "That's funny," we kept hearing him say, a
little behind us. "Somebody must have been along here
recently and gathered it all." Then we stifled our giggles,
the Walsh kids and myself, for once we'd found out what
to look for, we were scampering along ahead of him and
getting it all first. At the bottom of the mountain we presented him with a bagful that lasted him for years. The
taste? You love it or you hate it — but, like Libby, you can
develop a liking. You can find spruce gum not only on a
spruce tree, but in various New England stores — try the
Shelburne Country Store, Shelburne, Vermont — or by
writing to C. A. McMahan Co., Five Islands, Maine. It's
about fifteen cents a box; and I buy it by the carton.
Tamarack gum off a tamarack tree is even better, but I
don't recommend pine gum. It won't hurt you but you'll
never get it off your teeth. I've not tried hemlock gum,
after what happened to Socrates. And for an entirely
different taste and texture, chew a handful of raw wheat
grains, until you get down to the wheat gum.

I recommend also that you seek out ordinary staff-of-life
food, but the first-rate instead of the third-rate stuff that

we're all so accustomed to that we don't know any better. I wonder if certain first-rate foods even exist anymore. It's been a long time since I've eaten a really eggy egg. Our tastes get dulled by the poor, the standardized. Bread! One weeps to think what's happened to most bread:

> There's a huge bread factory near our house and I love to walk by it and just smell, it smells so wonderful, but then when you taste it, it's awful.
>
> — Jeff, grade 4

The cotton batting that you can roll into a bread-pill the size of a marble! Seek out new bread, hot, homemade, fresh-baked new bread, with high-quality butter. And thick, oozing hamburgers rather than the cardboard slabs you get at Freddie's. Try fresh-picked peas and strawberries. I went into a Howard Johnson's once, which had mammoth posters up all over the restaurant, extolling June and Feature-of-the-Month, STRAWBERRIES! in all forms from shortcake to ice cream. I inquired from the waitress if the berries were fresh picked, and she said no. It turned out they were making shortcake and sundaes from the same frozen strawberries they used all the other eleven months of the year!

Of course, all interesting tastes aren't eating tastes, or even good tastes, but to be a writer you have to be willing to sacrifice something for your Art. There's worm medicine. There's alum. As a small girl I put a penny in my mouth once, in church, and just about vomited — there's another taste — from the foul copper. I didn't have the courage to push past all those knees and bowed heads and go wash out my mouth, either.

Our daughters are woods-nibblers. They inherit this from grandparents, parents, and a book that's one of our bibles, *Stalking the Wild Asparagus*, by Euell Gibbons, which describes the pleasure of gathering and eating foods growing in the wild. The girls early discovered wintergreen leaves, which grow close to the ground with little glossy leaves and are used to flavor gum and toothpaste. They keep the dried leaves in their rooms at home in the winter. They taste everything — with the exception of unfamiliar mushrooms and berries. As they walk they pluck leaves, twigs, grasses, and crush, sniff, and sample. Sometimes the taste is interesting and worth swallowing, often it is not.

My sister Pat used to prepare "taste thrills" for me. I soon became wise enough not to respond when she chanted, "Open your mouth and shut your eyes, I'll give you something to make you wise," or was it "and you will get a big surprise"? Same difference. I myself made up tasty concoctions for my goat, mixtures of various cow feeds and pig formulas, but Sugarpuss always preferred straight oats and elm leaves, which she ate with much waggling of the tail. She also like cigarettes and my brother's used clarinet reeds, but not tin cans. That's a goat myth. She just liked the paper labels off them.

Next advice: couple your tasting with your writing. It's challenging to describe tastes, as I found out when I tried to describe spruce gum. Thomas Jefferson, a man of many talents and fine-honed tastes, didn't merely write the Declaration of Independence and the Preamble to the Constitution. He also wrote, "On a hot day in Virginia I know of nothing more comforting than a fine spiced pickle, brought up trout-like from the sparkling depths of that aromatic jar below stairs in Aunt Sally's cellar."

Kenneth Grahame describes taste in terms of the other senses: the garlic *sang*, cheese *lay down and cried*. That shows you it wasn't any old pasteurized processed cheese product from the supermarket, it was the real McCoy. Other books that have fun with food are *Green Eggs and*

Ham, Bread and Jam for Frances — that's all she'll eat —
and *An Anteater Named Arthur,* who gets tired of the same
old guess-what's-for-breakfast every morning. And don't
forget the chapter in *Caddie Woodlawn* where she and her
brothers become so tired of turkey sandwiches that they
trade for the half-breed children's buckets of parched corn.

Then besides describing tastes, those you like and those
you don't, write down your own stories that deal with
taste. Probably our best and funniest, the most vivid and
interesting writing, will be the negative ones dealing with
food.

Food's so absolutely basic. A psychologist states matter-
of-factly, "Since giving food is giving love . . ." As parents
we withhold food as a punishment *(Where the Wild Things
Are);* give it as a reward; stuff ourselves when we feel
unloved; we sometimes get huffy when children reject our
meals, i.e., our love. With food so often used for manipu-
lation, no wonder children's, and everybody's taste buds
get confused. Our simple Rat-and-Mole pleasure in the
good things of life becomes complicated. Dr. Spock was
forced to eat squash once as a child; it was forty years
before he tried it again, and discovered that he liked it.

My husband was force-fed as a child, and grew up
hating meal times. As a result we've bent over the other
way and never make our girls eat, although I occasionally
get mad or put the screws on them. I was only forced to
eat once, and remember clearly sitting for what seemed
hours in front of that bowl of creamed cauliflower, until
Mittens our cat came by and I fed it to her.

A friend of ours poured her orange juice through a knothole in the floor every morning, down to the dirt floor of
the cellar, where it sank in, until one morning she was
careless and poured it on top of her mother who was down
there doing the wash.

Another friend ate at a huge, round oak table which

weighed a ton, and when her mother finally moved it to spring-houseclean, down cascaded a year's worth of bread crusts which Meg had been secretly tucking on an inside ledge.

A final story: a couple of years ago I came across a box of chocolate-covered insects at a gourmet store. I thought it'd be a good joke to give them to the kids, they'd have fun taking them to school and showing their friends. So I bought the box and wrapped it and put it under the Christmas tree. I'll let Megan proceed, for she read this bit and informed me scathingly I had it all wrong. Actually, she should start sooner: I'd written, "You could see the bees in the candies, and the ants," and she wrote in the margin, "You *couldn't!* They were wrapped in tinfoil and even when you opened it you could only see *ants.*" Well, as she continues:

"We opened the box together and we all selected one. Jill, baby bee, me, caterpillar, Demi, ants. Jill and I unwrapped ours and ate them in one bite. They were good, crunchy like malted milk.

"Demi said, 'They're real.'

"We laughed. 'They're malted milk,' *we* said, and we argued a bit but Demi showed us hers — indeed, *ants,* that hadn't been covered — floating mangled on hard chocolate. We were stricken but it was *done,* and after all, they *were* good. (It was too late for the sink, both of us had swallowed.)"

That last sentence was because in my account I had Jill running to wash her mouth out when she discovered her mistake. It just goes to show that if the event happens to you, your memory is apt to be more accurate than other people's, even your mother's. In defense I hasten to add that I didn't expect the girls to think the chocolate-covered insects were fake, and eat them, although there are, of course, cultures such as the Australian aborigines that relish insects. And Saint John there in the wilderness lived on locusts and wild honey; it always used to turn my stomach, back in Sunday School, to think of him munching down those creatures like potato chips.

What are your stories? As a guest, did you ever choke down something you didn't like? Or have to eat another meal right after you'd already eaten? Arrive somewhere expecting dinner and not gotten it, and in your mind gone over every shelf of the refrigerator at home, as your hunger increased? One fourth-grader wrote that he swallowed a lump in his orange juice, and his mother told him it was a goldfish. "Would my own mother deceive me?" he queried. It turned out that she'd emptied the liquid remaining in a can of peaches into the orange juice, and a bit of peach had gone along. Now there's a mother I can relate to!

You also might try broadening your "taste empathy" by putting yourself in the place of an animal, as E. B. White did with Charlotte, Wilbur, and Templeton. Write about their lives from their point of view, including their diet. And by all means, whether you are writing about animals, yourself, or imaginary creatures from a distant galaxy, describe food and other tastes through *all* the senses. See if you can make your cheese lie down and cry. Your garlic sing.

10

Me Best Thoughts

From the diary of an Irish girl, published in 1940 as *The Book of Maggie Owen:*

> January 24, 1908. This is me birthday and I consider me New Year begins this day instead of January first. Anyways I was given this book for a present and a gold soverign along with it, a prayer book also that I have too many of. I start this book this day and shall put down me best thoughts and all important things that happen to me — if any do — and what I learn at me lessons. I call it a Year Book instead of a Diary because diary sounds like a running

off of the bowels and is vulgar. Me name is Marget Owen, a fine name would anyone call it me. Always they call me Maggie-Ane or Peg, I don't know why Owen is called Ane. I think theres many a thing I'll have to find out.

From Demi's journal, at age fourteen:

Grandma has just gone through 10 years of Great Aunt Jessie's diaries and found absolutely nothing worth saving in them. They just said things like, "went to Dougans for dinner today," "cold and snowy," "great-grandma died today," and never showed any of her feelings or even had more than a sentence on anything that happened so they just threw them out. I would bore myself silly if I kept something like that. What's the use of even writing it?

From Megan's journal, seventh grade:

And I got mad and said I *was* doing my work with good spirits and you just wrecked them, and Mom yelled, well do your math anyway, immediately. And I yelled stop it, I felt like kicking her, I wanted to leave this stupid old place forever. I think I'm going to be a mental wreck if this keeps up. I wish I had a lock for my door. I wish school was out and this was over. Eight more weeks of all this. I'd like to swear but I'd get in trouble. KIDS NEED PLACES TO VENT THEIR ANGER! Grownups don't understand that. They can run around stomping and yelling at kids and swearing and stuff but we can't. We need something to yell at, especially parents. WE HAVE TO HAVE MORE THAN BOOKS TO WRITE OUR ANGER IN! I'M GOING TO GIVE MY KIDS AN ANGER ROOM OR SOMETHING! . . .

From Megan's journal, eighth grade:

. . . I hope I mean something to somebody. How about Elspeth's friends? Am I a stupid older sister to them — like my friends' older sisters were to me? What a disgusting thought. I really don't want to spend my time impressing them. . . . The grownups are involved in impressing each other — and just by living they impress us. The little kids are so far away from the grownups they can hardly see beyond their parents. The grownups do not try to impress us but they do.

We struggle to impress the grownups — like dogs wanting a pat on the head. Attention from a grownup we admire is sheer bliss — complete happiness. We also want to impress each other. I don't remember so well about when I was little. Maybe I did look up to older kids, maybe not. But from now on I think I'll watch more closely to see if anybody is trying to impress me, and if they are, be impressed. And love them. . . .

From Jill's journal, at age eleven or twelve:

Hear

Birds
Frodo's tags jingling
Frodo yawning
Elspeth humming
cars in the distance
petals falling on the book
wind in the branches

Feel

bark on my knee
pen in my hand
lid to pen in my other hand
paper
clothes
hair on my arm

Taste

pen cap — blasé
apple blossom petals —
    tart but good
apple leaves — bitter
paper — dry and tasteless

See

lilacs   car   sandpile
apple blossems   driveway
house   dirt   garage
trailer   paper   river
garden   pen   Frodo
wagon   me   grass

95

Smell

apple blossem   I'm up in the apple tree. writing. doing
paper   nothing but looking, listening, feeling, tast-
ink   ing, smelling, and moving my hand. every-
bark   thing is beautiful today. yesterday the
mud   world was washed. we had a tremendous
                 thunder storm. it was beautiful. me and
megan danced around in it, and got completely sopped. it
was great fun. mom and dad are gone so we are having lots
of freedom. i suppose i've been up here maybe half an hour.
I wish i could bead a head band and wear a feather, but i
don't have any beads. cruel. I should go down and find my
pen cap. i just lost it. vis: dropped it.

Eavesdropped conversation:

Megan: "I'll hate it! I won't go! It's so stupid to get all
dressed up and go to dancing class and learn to dance with
boys!"

Demi: "Oh, go ahead! It's only an hour a week and think
of all you'll have to write in your record book, all about
sweaty palms and how awful you feel. That's what record
books are for."

From Demi's journal, at age twelve or thirteen:

Things to do in a record book:

write things that happen
thoughts
feelings
ideas
make up stories or poems
copy poems that I like
observe other people and other things
list things that I hear — conversations
list of noises at one time
place

smells
feel of things
draw
copy things of interest
identifying trees, etc.
list of things to do
play games
eat pages
anything at all
I need not be so narrow minded

Another eavesdropped conversation:

Elspeth: What are you writing?
Megan: I'm writing in my Journal.
Elspeth: I know that, but are you writing about life, or a poem, or what?

Journals. Record books. Demi has filled eleven or twelve, Megan maybe seven, Jill about three, and Elspeth, in first grade, has begun her first. We buy actual books (and a proper book is important!) at an office supplies store or the stationery counter in a dime store. These say *Record Book* in gold letters on the black cover, and they have an elegant red binding. They're not notebooks but real volumes, solidly bound, and have blank lined pages. They cost in the neighborhood of a dollar, depending on store and size. The girls like the 5½" by 8" book best, which fits comfortably into the rear pocket of bib overalls. Jill even has "Record Book" embroidered on one rear pocket, and "Basil" on the narrow pocket on the bib which holds her favorite checkerboarded pencil.

This chapter had its origin a couple of years ago as a discussion over the radio between the two older girls and myself. Jill wasn't a participant because at the time she hadn't fully caught the record book habit. Her single volume contained only a few pages of writing and a rather

97

intricate map. Megan, then thirteen, began the program by challenging me, "If you're so hot on everybody keeping journals, Mom, how come you never kept any when you were little?"

My defense was that I had tried, but I had kept the wrong sort. I was given plenty of diaries, but instead of being a running off of the bowels as Maggie Owen says, they acted more like constipation. I'd lose the diary, and lie in bed recalling what I'd done January fifth, sixth, and seventh. The next night it would be January fifth, sixth, seventh, and eighth, so as to get all events down accurately when I found it. It was like the game where you take something beginning with A in your valise, the next player takes A and B, and each succeeding player has to remember the whole rigmarole in order. The sheer weight of remembering, and also of guilt — for I felt as though the diary was something I *had* to do — killed diaries for me. I said that day on the radio that I'd given each of my children a record book in hopes of freeing them to write rather than imposing rules and regulations that might block them, as diaries did me.

Demi agreed that the date did make a person feel obliged. "If you miss a day, there's that blank space staring at you. Also most diaries just give you a tiny space to write in and by the time you say, 'It snowed out today, and I got an E on this exam,' it's all filled up. But in our blank record books you can draw pictures or copy a recipe or do anything you want to. You don't have to write in it every day; you can write pages and pages, and then maybe not again for a week. I didn't even mark down dates when I first started keeping journals, but now I do, so that I can figure out what's going on. Because a lot of times I don't write things in order. Also, when I go back and read an old journal, I find I like to know when it was and without dates it's sometimes hard to tell."

I said, "I think if I'd had a record book I would have done a lot more of the kind of writing you kids have done, and that I wish I'd done. More of an autobiography."

Megan didn't quite agree. "I think of *autobiography* as writing about yourself all the time, 'I did this' and 'I did that,' but you can put so much *more* in a record book. But I guess when you think about it it's all a record of you, actually."

Demi: "That's because when you write in a poem you like or draw a picture, that poem is part of you. It just tells about you in a different sort of way."

I asked Demi if she could find a poem to read to me. She said, "Well, here's one by Megan. I asked her to write something in my record book and she wrote a poem:

> *Smoke is nice.*
> *It comes out in a stream*
> *And spreads out in single lines*
> *Until it is completely spread*
> *Like a drop of paint in a glass of water*
> *And a single breath*
> *Disturbs the perfect film*
> *Into many."*

"That was watching incense," said Megan. "In the tent."

We went back to autobiography. I observed that the ones I'd read had a habit of being written later, in composure, toward the end of a life or after an interesting phase. The writer reflects on the significant movements of his life and how they all fit together —

"Or don't," Megan interrupted.

"But a journal," I continued, "is going on at the time, a sort of running autobiography. It captures the small things which are the seeds of later reflective autobiography. Demi's "ih" poem, all the woody type poems and incidents.

99

But you mentioned rereading your journals, Demi. Why do you do this? And how does it make you feel? Do you sound like *you*?"

"Sometimes I do and sometimes I don't. Sometimes it gives me a new perspective on who I am. Sometimes when you are just living everyday life you forget other things that have happened. It's as if you have forgotten pieces of yourself."

I said, "The past is apt to get a sort of smoothness, like looking back along a long grayish road — or it flattens out like hilly ground seen from an airplane. Yet with the incidents recorded in your books you'll be reminded that it was richly punctuated: you were in a thundering rage, or you had this delicate thought or that restless itching. Life had its mountains and valleys, and even its little humps and hollows weren't without interest, and also its trees and stumps and flowers and poison ivy. Do you have any 'Early Demi' you'd let us hear?"

Demi:

"The crows were in the cemetery again today. My bus must have come early because I started out in plenty of time and I had just crossed the road when it turned the corner. I laid down in the snow so they wouldn't see and wait for me. The snow was very damp and wet. I feel dumb running such a distance while the people on the bus watch me. I reminded myself of a rabbit crouching stilly till the danger passed. Last time I just stood motionless and they thought they saw someone and waited awhile. I am a bit larger than a rabbit."

Me: "Aha! Some of those mornings I had to drive you to school were hoaxes! But I can empathize — I used to be embarrassed to run to the school taxi, too. I remember walking along swinging my belt, trying to appear very nonchalant and not speeding up at all and then when I got there George would bellow, 'WHY DIDN'T YOU RUN?' And speaking of embarrassment, I talked to your Aunt Jo about diaries and journals once, after we were grown up and she noticed you kids keeping yours. She said she'd always destroyed her diaries shortly after she'd written them because when she got to reading back over them she'd be so embarrassed at what she had been the year before, how dumb she was, or how silly, what stupid things she was interested in, that she'd rip them up."

Megan: "I'm embarrassed, sometimes, but I don't wreck them or anything."

Demi: "Usually I like looking back because it makes me realize I *was* different. And if I'm really bored sometimes it's interesting to go back and find other things that have happened, things I was interested in that I'd forgotten about and things I can do again, or that remind me of fresh things."

Me: "But do you feel embarrassed when you see something that you think was silly of you, or do you smile and say, 'Little Demi thought that was important, and now I see that it really isn't, very, but it was to me at the time'? Do you have those feelings?"

Demi: "Both!"

Me: "This is what I think Aunt Jo needed more of; a respect for what she had been, some sort of perspective to say, 'Yes, those were the concerns of a nine- or eleven-year-old, and now that I'm thirteen I shouldn't despise what I was interested in or the sorts of things that I wrote then.' A compassion for her younger self."

Megan: "It's even worse when it's closer. If you look at what you wrote last year it's more embarrassing than something you wrote when you were nine."

Me: "You have less distance."

Demi: "I think part of my writing is so that I'll remember what it's like to be young when I'm ninety years old."

Me: "This is what I wish I'd done. I was busy writing

stories of the faraway and fantastic, fairies and Oz and talking rabbits, which was okay, but I wish I'd also been writing down what I was thinking about at nine, and the things I noticed, or did, or felt, or thought were important, or even didn't think were important. All those areas are lost to me except through memory. The actual comments, the voice of my ten-year-old past speaking out to me. In a journal of yours, Demi, last year I think, you showed me a passage:

> Megan got HMS Pinafore yesterday and we are observing a respite by sitting on the rug in the window alcove and listening to the record. A carton of frozen A&P SLICED STRAWBERRIES occupies a position of prominence in the center of our triangle. Jill is crosslegged in the Bean-chair doing Math homework. She is struggling to chew gum between bites of strawberry but the gum tends to chill quickly when not in use. Megan was writing but is now ensconsed in a book Mom handed her to judge. (*Wiley and the Hairy Man.*) I am crosslegged in Dad's paisley P.J.'s with wet hair. . . . Pinafore is like being with a very old friend whom you are comfortable with without speaking.

I'd give a lot for some scenes like that about my own childhood. Nothing earthshaking, but *alive*. It never occurred to me to write them down."

Demi: "You don't expect to forget the usual, yet that's the first thing you do."

Me: "What about privacy? Diaries often come with locks; record books don't, and you leave yours lying around all the time."

Megan: "I didn't used to care that much, but the last year or so I've wanted mine private, and that's why I was so mad when Jill read mine all the way through. My record book is a door into me, and I don't want people in except by invitation. Or they can at least knock. Jill broke in and

— and *vandalized*. I felt like an oyster, all opened up and shriveling."

Me: "Well, the way I heard it, you read hers first —"

Megan: "Not *technically!* She left hers lying open and there was the line staring right up at me, 'I read Megan's record book and it was boring.' So I went and beat her up."

Demi: "For me it depends on the person. If somebody asks, 'Can I read it?' I wonder, did I write anything about you? If so is it good or bad? But I really enjoyed reading sections to Uncle Bill that one time."

Megan: "That's what happened to *Harriet the Spy*. She had all those spy notebooks, sort of like our record books —"

Me: "I sometimes refer to your books as 'Harriet note-books.' "

Megan: "— and her friends got ahold of them and were really mad."

Me: "I confess I'm tempted occasionally to take a peek into your books, because I find them so interesting — and when, like Jill's, you leave them open on the tank of the toilet, that's too much to expect any human being to resist —"

Megan: "Just *sneaky* human beings!"

Me: "— but I don't think I've ever used anything I've read against any of you. It helps me to understand you better."

Megan: "I don't want understanding. I want *privacy!*"

Me: "As the March Hare said, 'Suppose we change the subject!' Demi, even though you don't feel compelled to write daily, do you still have some cycle of regularity?"

Demi: "Sometimes I find I have lapses of longer than a month and then I think well, I'm not writing because I *have* to, and so I just shouldn't feel guilty — but sometimes I do, anyway."

Me: "Any reason for the lapses?"

Demi: "Sometimes a lot of things happen. Once you get behind you feel as though you want to keep remembering those things, yet you never get them down so you're afraid to begin new things because you don't want to forget the old. After a while they all pile up and you just have to forget all of them and begin fresh. Because there are so many things that you miss and can't write about anyway. . . . Sometimes it's very hard to write about feelings. . . . Or if you're with a lot of people it's hard to explain the circumstances. You need to describe each person and there is so much that you have to know by sight and feel that it takes so long to write."

Me: "Don't you also find that when you're actively engaged in something it's hard to step aside and write about it? If you have a period of, say, several weeks where you are being very much involved with people and activities without much time for writing and reflection?"

Demi: "I thought a while back that only my middling feelings got in my journals because at times of great excitement or strong feelings I wasn't writing, but then I began looking and discovered that there were plenty of occasions where I remembered those feelings well enough to get them in!"

Megan: "I write when I'm mad at somebody. Or glad with somebody. Whenever I'm in a strong mood. Or else when I'm bored or lonely and haven't anything to do. Or when I'm out on the lake in the canoe."

Demi: "I write a lot of things in the canoe, too. They all begin, 'All these motorboats are trying to tip me over!' "

Me: "Journals, of course, are a valid form of literature. You've read in English class parts of *Pepys' Diary* — he puts in whether his dinner agreed with him, and how he pinches the servant girls, as well as cataclysmic things, such as the Great Fire. It's the details about matters large or small that make any journal interesting to read."

Megan: "And Grandpa and Grandma have been reading all the journals of what's-his-name that followed Dr. Johnson around —"

Me: "Boswell. People used to think the principal value of those journals was what Boswell said about Johnson, but now Boswell is recognized as a major literary figure in his own right, on account of them."

Demi: "One thing about writing journals, you don't have to worry about the plot!"

Megan: "Or the characters."

Me: "Often there's a natural plot in the unfolding of life. And a lot more drama than people would believe!"

Demi: "Even in an ordinary life."

Me: "Yes, lots of not-so-famous journals of not-at-all-important people are fascinating. And even line-a-day diaries have at least historical value — the pinpointing of events — or an occasional illuminating bit —"

Megan: "Sure, tell about the time we ate with that man at the Pancake House. He was working on journals; the Civil War soldier who on the day the South captured him just wrote, 'Surrounded by rebels and taken captive. Marched six miles to camp. Slept on the ground. Very cold.' He died a prisoner, too; his diary was sent home."

Me: "Yes, that was one of our best discussions, the night we were eating out with Gram and Gramp, and Judge Luebke joined us. Demi, you started it all because you were writing in your journal while waiting to be served, and he asked what you were doing."

Megan: "And Judge Luebke said he was collecting diaries and journals from early settlers right around Beloit and Janesville — there was that one where the man said what a pretty and cultured town Beloit was, but Janesville up the river was just a rude settlement with a bunch of uncouth people!"

Demi: "You had me read aloud that part of my journal

where I wrote about Great Aunt Jessie's diaries — how Grandma thought she'd discovered a great treasury of family chronicles after Jessie died, but there wasn't anything in them, even of historical value."

Me: "And I recall asking whether anyone knew the books *American Diaries,* and *British & Scottish Diaries.* I discovered those when I was working on the Irish Famine book."

Megan: "When are you going to get around to writing that book?"

Me: "I don't know. Maybe when somebody pays my way to Ireland. But I thought I could learn a lot about Ireland at the time of the famine, and crossing the Atlantic in 1850, if I could find some authentic records. Those books are a listing of all the diaries the editors could locate; what was the nature of each diary; and where they can be looked at. Some interesting stuff — they listed diaries as famous as Pepys and Boswell, and also one that was only one sentence long, by a twelve-year-old girl, but was such a good sentence that they included it."

Demi: "Jill's journal may be famous yet!"

Megan: "Except it's not good enough!"

Me: "Also the diaries seemed to fall into regular categories. Travel diaries — people setting out on trips would suddenly take to keeping one. Social diaries, usually by prominent wives, listing the guests at such and such a party, what was served, and so forth. Spiritual diaries, often clergymen's but not always, of the wrestlings of their souls with the devil. Then there were the general diaries, more like your journals. But there were a few pretty unique ones — such as the poisoner's diary. He kept in it the names of his victims, what poison he administered and when, and a description of the death throes of the victim, if he was able to witness them. It was through his journal that they convicted him."

Demi: "I thought you couldn't testify against yourself!"

Me: "I don't know the fine points of the law, but better watch what you write! And another category listed was children's diaries. These are a valid form of literature, too, and I'm sure are published more often than any other works by children, not counting the stuff in the children's magazines. They're read by adults as well as children. You've both liked the anthology of passages from children's diaries called *Small Voices*."

Demi: "And also *The Book of Maggie Owen* and *Maggie No Doubt*."

Me: "Sure, we've all loved Maggie, and there's Anne Frank's diary, and a book that filled me with jealousy when I was ten, called *Around the World in Eleven Years*, by Patience, Richard, and John Abbe. Patience was eleven and did all the writing though —"

Megan: "Why jealousy?"

Me: "Well, she had hard covers and I'd only been printed in a newspaper, and every time she referred to herself she didn't say 'I' but 'I, Patience,' and I felt that was very bad literary style to keep reminding the reader of her name all the time when we knew perfectly well who was writing the book."

Demi: "It probably spurred you on and kept you writing."

Me: "But not journals. . . ."

Megan: "What about *O Ye Jigs and Juleps*, by Virginia somebody?"

Me: "That's a good one. Those were essays for her English teacher, but are exactly like journal entries except she chooses a subject and discusses it, like sin. And then goes on to relate in happy detail all the ways she's been bad and will probably go to Hell. Journals can be *imagined*, too, as a form of literature. A story is often deliberately told in the form of a journal."

Demi: "The way I did in fifth grade social studies. I pretended I was Sarepta Blodgett — I found her name in that *Centennial Book of Beloit*, it said she and her sister Orinda came from Ohio to Wisconsin in a covered wagon."

Me: "Did you find that keeping journals yourself helped you to put in the type of details that made Sarepta's diary seem authentic?"

Demi: "Yes, and I really enjoyed doing that. I even made the journal look real. I wrote it with a fountain pen and made blots on purpose all over the place, and when she was writing in the wagon I made sure the lines were all bumpy and scratched and hard to read."

Me: "As a writer, *I* see a lot of value in journals, and I guess as a recommendation to young writers, any writers, my urging them to keep a journal is the most important advice I could give them. Journals incorporate everything else: the awareness of sights, sounds, feelings, one's self, everything gets sharpened and deepened. You're constantly practicing writing. You're providing a tremendous source of raw material for both now and later. You're compiling an invaluable family chronicle. And as a person beyond a writer, I feel what you're writing is a balm to the soul in many ways. But two final questions: No amount of parental pressure in the world could keep you girls writing on journals unless you really wanted to, unless you got something out of it. Why did you start to write in a journal? And why do you keep on?"

Demi: "I started because when I was little, I didn't want to forget what it was like to be a kid. When you're grown up you lose track of what kids know at different ages. They expect you to know so much less than you know. And also, I wanted to remember the types of thoughts you have when you're different ages. To remember the way I was looking at the world at twelve or whatever."

Megan: "I don't know . . . partly because Demi did. . . ."

Demi: "And because you needed something to be really vehement with?"

Megan: "Not in sixth grade! I don't know why. But last spring, when I lost my record book and waited and waited for someone to return it, and finally started a new one, I realized how much it meant to me:

> I have not written in a record book for a long, long time. Even as I have barely begun this one — 3 lines no more — I am filled with a sort of bubbling delight and I wonder why I waited so long for my other to be returned. I did not realize how I've missed it until now. Poems, letters and stories just do not satisfy me the way this does. I pity those who have not discovered record books, but who either confine themselves to diaries, or simply forget what happens. Feelings are much too important to be forgotten, and often times I think I do not think about myself enough.
>
> The canoe glides silently across the water. We are Indians in chase of the palefaces — Jerry.
>
> Beavers are met. They swim from the island to the point. With a sudden ker-PLUNK of their tails they swim — underwater — as fast as they can go — home.
>
> There is mist on the top of the Knob. It rises in slow swirls like a forest fire. The paddles have a soothing drip drip drip drip splash. . . ."

Me: "And the final question —"

Megan: "Hey, you asked your two!"

Me: "The first was a compound question. The last is, and maybe you've answered it already: I've noticed that your journals are very important to you, you don't go anyplace without them, and when they're lost there's a great scramble till they're found again. And your friends who have picked up the habit from you have the same attachment. The books seem to be a form of security, a Linus blanket. When Harriet couldn't write in her notebook they ended up taking her to a psychiatrist. Do you think your journals harm you in any way, that you retreat into them when maybe you should be outgoing, say, with friends or parents?"

Megan: "I discovered on the hiking trip that my journal *was* a Linus blanket! The night I left it in my pack I felt strange and rather defenseless, if anything happened. . . . Then the next night I kept it under my head and my sleeping bag kept sliding down and I kept reaching up to see if it was still there —"

Demi: "I didn't even take mine. . . . I did take pencil and paper, though, and later Scotch-taped in what I'd written. Usually I take it; I like having it along. It's nicer than regular paper. You lose regular paper. I guess it's been a Linus blanket a lot of the time."

Me: "But do you see any harm in that?"

Megan: "I see *good*. We're getting what we need, and we'll come across them years later in a musty old attic. *Your* musty old attic."

Me: "But do you retreat —"

Megan: "No! I don't retreat into my journal, I bring it along."

Demi: "If anything, if I retreat into my journal I become more *aware*, though I might lose some spur-of-the-moment time. Mostly I don't write spur-of-the-moment. I'm not terribly Harrietish. I can wait."

Megan: "I'm not that Harrietish, either."

11

Toast that Talks

. . . very hot buttered toast, cut thick, very brown on both
sides, with the butter running through the holes in it in great
golden drops, like honey from the honeycomb. The smell of
that buttered toast simply talked to Toad. . . .

— From *The Wind in the Willows*,
by Kenneth Grahame

KENNETH GRAHAME AGAIN, this time on smelling. When
I was fourteen or so I went through all my books and
marked "F.B." inside the covers of my favorites. *The Wind
in the Willows* got an "F.B." with four stars. When you
read it you can't help but feel that the whole book is a
celebration of just being alive. The book is dripping with
the golden drops of touching, tasting, sniffing, gazing,
listening, and the less tangible inner senses of awe, wander-
lust, homing, friendship, God, beauty, love, joy, contentment. Every page is as aquiver with awareness as Mole's

moist nose. It is like the gypsy stew which the escaping
Toad smells when he is famished:

> A fire of sticks was burning nearby, and over the fire
> hung an iron pot, and out of that pot came forth bubblings
> and gurglings, and a vague suggestive steaminess. Also
> smells — warm, rich, and varied smells — that twined and
> twisted and wreathed themselves at last into one complete,
> voluptuous, perfect smell that seemed like the very soul of
> nature taking form and appearing to her children, a true
> Goddess, a mother of solace and comfort.

Smell, like taste, is another of the more neglected senses.
Compared to animals we don't smell particularly well. You
notice I didn't say *good* — although people are preoccupied
with their own odors. With ourselves the smell's divided
into two camps: we want to smell nice, and so the perfume
ads; we don't want to smell bad, hence the deodorant ones.
I rather like the smell of sweat, myself. Ordinarily, however, we aren't much aware of our sense of smell as an aid
to perception. Not so with Grahame's animals:

> We others, who have long lost the more subtle of the
> physical senses, have not even proper terms to express an
> animal's intercommunications with his surroundings, living
> or otherwise, and have only the word "smell," for instance,
> to include the whole range of delicate thrills which murmer
> in the nose of the animal night and day, summoning, warn-
> ing, inciting, repelling. It was one of these mysterious fairy
> calls from out of the void that suddenly reached Mole in the
> darkness, making him tingle through and through with its
> very familiar appeal, even while as yet he could not clearly
> remember what it was. He stopped dead in his tracks, his
> nose searching hither and thither in its efforts to recap-
> ture the fine filament, and telegraphic current, that had so
> strongly moved him. A moment, and he had caught it again;
> and with it this time came recollection in the fullest flood.

Home! That was what they meant, those caressing appeals, those soft touches wafted through the air, those invisible little hands pulling and tugging, all one way!

To me the sense of smell has an elusive quality, a primitive, evocative quality to a greater degree than the other senses. Once in a great while I get a whiff and something powerful, compelling, unknown, wells up out of the past over me. I grasp at it, try to hold the moment long enough to identify it; it's linked with an emotion of tremendous depth, maybe beauty, and it's there for an instant, unrelated to anything in the *now*. *What is it?* If I could catch its meaning I would understand — what? Something awfully important. But like a wave it pulls back and is gone. I think it is this quality that Kipling is referring to when he says, "Smells are surer than sounds or sights to make your heart strings crack." And I think that this is an experience you don't have to be old to have, either; the little fingers clutching Mole can clutch a child.

The experience is described more scientifically in an item I tore out of some magazine a few years ago:

> Ever notice how a sudden aroma can bridge decades and distances instantaneously and make you recall vividly events of your early childhood? How a special flavor sets off a whole train of nostalgic reminiscences? It's probably because your scent memory, closely allied to taste, probably reaches farther back than any other type of memory. It's surprisingly acute and its scope is vast. You can distinguish up to ten thousand different odors. In childhood your senses were even keener and each new odor registered indelibly. It takes only a hair-trigger stimulus to set this memory in motion: specifically, only one five-hundred-millionth part of a milligram in 50 cc. of air.

What are my favorite smells? Ross Parmenter once asked us, in a game where we gave many of our "favorites," "What do you like best to smell?" I pondered, and at my turn replied, "Manure on the fields in spring." This was greeted with hoots, howls, and exaggerated gagging by the various-age children present, and though that particular batch of kids is now all grown they still, when they whiff a manure-laden wind, exclaim, "Oh, there's Jackie's smell." A more acceptable smell I might have chosen would have been my grandparents' cellar. I'd go down there for the sole purpose of sniffing. Not in the furnace section (acrid) nor the canned goods closet (dusty) but in the root cellar where the floor was unpaved and the walls earthen, where there were bins of potatoes, carrots buried in sand, bushels of turnips and of apples: Jonathans and Winesaps and Pippins all blending their pungency with the damp earth. I didn't know that word, pungent, at the time, but discovered later that it partly describes the fragrance, though not the whole heady experience. And a pungent, rich, heavy, earthy odor is what manure-on-fields is, too, or the odor described on a scrap of paper I found on the floor a few years ago, in Demi's handwriting, and saved: "The wormy smell of rain."

There's another interesting property to smell. Your eyes or ears can become unseeing or unhearing but by an act of will you can make them register again. The same with touch and taste. But a continuous smell on our olfactory nerves, or whatever it is we smell with, deadens them and diminishes the odor. My discovery of this involves another manure story:

When we were kids the manure and straw would be allowed to pile up in the calf barn over the winter. Fresh straw would just be thrown on top of it. I learned later, from *Charlotte's Web*, that manure as it decomposes keeps the animals warm and so there is a reason for keeping it in the barns; it's not just bad housekeeping. Anyway, come spring, some of the hired men were pitching the manure out of the calf barn and the stench was terrible. It was stronger than even I could bear, and we kids dared each other to go in the barn and see who could stand it longest. So we all marched in, holding our noses, but gradually began talking to the men and to each other, and became interested in other things. After a while someone suddenly remembered that we were there on a dare. This is why I guess people can endure living in places that smell terrible. Their smelling apparatus gets numbed.

Certain smells are more deadening than others, and the recovery time of the nerves lengthier. I read a story once where the outcome of a murder trial depended on a certain man's sense of smell, and he was being tested by a series of distinctive scents in bottles to see whether he could indeed identify smells with the acuity he claimed. The clever lawyer gave him first a sniff of gasoline, and after that, he couldn't identify anything. The jury didn't know that gasoline could do this, and so the case was lost.

For improving our own smell sensitivity I recommend the lawyer's game. Use opaque bottles and jars, and see how many odors a group of you can identify. Try it again in a few weeks and see if you've improved. Spices are fine. Pencil shavings. Watch out for medicines and certain other strong smells; also beware how you smell something from an unknown bottle. You could sear your nasal passages, even kill yourself. A friend who is a nurse says she was taught at the hospital not to smell heavily, at the lip of a strange bottle, but to fan her hand over the top and whiff the breeze. To catch it on a glance. This technique I find improves a lot of nonharmful odors, such as perfume.

Another way to be more aware is to seek out scents. Wet mittens on a radiator. A root cellar. A bakery, a pharmacy, a welding shop, a calf barn. Harriet said that a hardware store smelled like an old thermos bottle.

Read about how others describe smell. In *The Story of*

Doctor Dolittle Jip the dog is asked to trace a man who uses Black Rapee snuff, when all the birds of the world have been unable to spot him. Jip says scornfully that this is an easy smell, mere pup's play, and he stands with his nose in the wind and tells as he sniffs:

"Tar, Spanish onions, kerosene oil, wet raincoats, crushed laurel-leaves, rubber burning, lace-curtains being washed — no, my mistake, lace-curtains hanging out to dry, and foxes — hundreds of 'em — cubs, and —"

"Can you really smell all those different things in this one wind?" asked the Doctor.

"Why, of course!" said Jip. "And those are only a few of the easy smells — the strong ones. Any mongrel could smell those with a cold in the head. Wait now, and I'll tell you some of the harder scents that are coming on this wind — a few of the dainty ones."

Then the dog shut his eyes tight, poked his nose straight up in the air and sniffed hard with his mouth half-open. . . .

"Bricks," he whispered, very low — "old yellow bricks, crumbling with age in a garden-wall; the sweet breath of young cows standing in a mountain-stream; the lead roof of a dove-cote — or perhaps a granary — with the midday sun on it; black kid gloves lying in a bureau-drawer of walnut-wood; a dusty road with a horses' drinking-trough beneath the sycamores; little mushrooms bursting through the rotting leaves; and — and — and —"

"Any parsnips?" asked Gub-Gub.

"No," said Jip. . . . "No parsnips whatever. . . ."

In *Charlotte's Web*, E. B. White describes Wilbur's barn:

The barn was very large. It was very old. It smelled of hay and it smelled of manure. It smelled of the perspiration of tired horses and the wonderful sweet breath of patient cows. It often had a sort of peaceful smell — as though nothing bad could happen ever again in the world. It smelled of grain and of harness dressing and of axle grease and of rubber boots and of new rope. And whenever the cat was given a fish-head to eat, the barn would smell of fish. But mostly it smelled of hay, for there was always hay in the great loft up overhead.

I lead with the nose in Libby's introduction to the Ran Pasture — the loggers' bunkroom — in *The Taste of Spruce Gum:*

> Libby followed [Mrs. Vincent] into a long room and wrinkled her nose.
> "Terrible smell, ain't it! What with their stinkin' pipes and clothes, and I don't think one of 'em's had a bath since their mother give 'em one — you oughta smell it here in the spring, when they're smearin' up their faces and necks with lard and kerosene to keep the black gnats from bitin'! 'Course we grease up the window frames too, but it don't do no good to keep 'em out, nasty things. Don't need no screens; flies don't come this high and the gnats'd go right through 'em. They're a right enough plague."
> "But the kerosene's strong *now,* as if it's been spilled over everything!"
> "So it has." Mrs. Vincent hurried down the aisle between two rows of wood bunks. . . . "Don't use no nightshirts. Sleep in their underwear, or when it's cold, in all their clothes. You just set them sheets down for now." Mrs. Vincent poured kerosene into the basin and took a feather off a ledge. She dipped it in the kerosene and began running the feather into the cracks of the headboard of the first stripped bed.
> Libby gaped.
> "Bedbugs," explained Mrs. Vincent. "Can't get rid of 'em, but at least kerosene keeps 'em under control. There's one!"

Here's bathing a sloth in *Julie's Secret Sloth:*

> The sloth sprawled awkwardly in the water but did not protest. Seizing the soap she worked up a greasy lather on his back. Sampson sat patiently. A fetid odor rose from his grayish hair and hung in the moist air — a stronger smell than her wool coat when it rained on Easter.

While I've never bathed a sloth, it's been my experience from sudsing up many reluctant dogs, a most reluctant rabbit — she'd leapt into my magenta oil paints — and a sheep, as well as various unwashed and hairy humans, that there is a common element to the smell of wet hair. So far, nobody's challenged me on a soaked sloth.

Here's a final quote that I find very interesting because it talks about lack-of-smell. It's from *Marianne Dreams*, a strange fantasy by Catherine Storr. Marianne draws, and when she dreams finds herself in her own picture, although she doesn't realize this for several dreams. Here she enters the house she has drawn:

> Marianne, as she came through the door, had felt certain, without knowing why, that the house was lived in. . . . It might have been a smell — because, although we very seldom realize it, we respond to smells a great deal more than we know; and the smell of an empty house is quite different from the smell of one that is lived in. This house had no smell, and this alone would have been extraordinary. It felt like those imitation houses which are put up for show or advertisement, in exhibitions or on the stage. Those houses have no smell: you could tell with your eyes shut and your hands tied behind you that they are not real and not only are not lived in, but never have been and never will be lived in. . . . But it wasn't the no-smell that Marianne noticed. Something else was contradicting the smell-lessness of the house and lack of furniture, the emptiness of the room and hall and the echoing sound of her footsteps. The something else was a sound, the regular ordinary tick of a clock.

Writing about smells will improve your smelling awareness, too. Describe scents as you encounter them or remember them. Make a list of smells you like. Fresh sheets on your bed that have been dried in the sun and wind? New-mown hay? Don't forget the smells you don't like, either; the disgusting ones, the stenches and stinks. A writer uses them all. I walked into Jill's fifth-grade class-room once, a mobile unit with no coat hall or lockers, and exclaimed to the kids, "Phew! This room smells like an old sweaty tennis shoe!" They pointed, and every one had a pair hanging by the shoelaces over the back of his or her chair.

Try for precise words that describe a particular smell: acrid, pungent, earthy, fragrant, fetid, putrid. What would you call the cutting smell of Vicks? I've still to find the right word for ammonia. I so loathed that smell as a child that I couldn't bring myself to use ammonia for cleaning until very recently.

For stories, when can you remember that you used your nose? For years I embarrassed my mother, especially out in company, by giving a sniff to all my food before I ate it — a necessary habit learned from swapping lunch-box sand-wiches. Another strong smell I recall from grade school is the trampled (often on purpose) stink bugs that were thick under the box elder tree by the kindergarten door. A further story idea: imagine yourself to be a keen-smelling animal, a dog for a day. I think your doggy nose, as con-trasted to your human one, would come suddenly into prominence, and not merely because it takes up most of your face.

And don't forget poems. Scents and smells have always been an important part of the poet's repertoire:

> I can always tell
> Which are Keats' clothes
> Because they smell
> Like Keats.
> I think I'm going to be able
> To sniff out
> My children
> When I'm a mommy.
> — Elspeth, age 6

At this point, I originally ended the chapter on smelling. Considerably later Megan read it, and thrust under my nose (appropriately) a page of notes. Since I obviously have an authority right in my own family, I feel I had better include her comments:

"MOM, YOU IGNORED PEOPLE-SMELLING TOO MUCH! HERE ARE SOME THOUGHTS.

"About the Keats poem, I can do it too. First, a family. I sniff a shirt, I smell the Perlmutters. I sniff again and I know it's Greg's. People sometimes get insulted when I tell them they smell. They say, 'Like *what*?' I say, 'Like yourself. I can't explain it, there's nothing to compare it to.' They still sometimes are cross with me, how could *they* smell? HORRORS! And I've never smelt anybody except Gary Stubbs who smelt bad! Or any two people who smelt alike. You know, there's doggy smell, but no two dogs smell just alike. Same with people. I like smelling people.

"What's hard is smelling yourself. Smell your bottom lip — pull it up under your nose. Mine smells like a baby. Does yours? Smell your old clothes. Wash them without soap so you wash away any sweat and dirt but not *you*. Smell your *pillow*.

"You're so used to your own, and your family smell that it's hard to realize. Smell your parents' pillows, your sisters' and brothers', your friends'. Maybe you will come to be able to tell them apart, and like smelling people, too."

End of Megan's comments, and I do think a paean on people-smelling makes a fitting grand finale. Matter of fact, I've been sniffing people a little more consciously myself, ever since she wrote it. But it's like the eavesdropping. You mustn't let them know you're doing it.

12

When She Was Bad,
She Was Horrid

Jon was the most mischievous boy in Parson's Court. He
could sink his father's shoes in the rainbarrel and not feel
guilty. So when he tied the three year old baby on a helium
balloon and let it go he only felt rather glad Benny was gone.

— From *Benny's Balloon*
by Gillian Jackson, age 10

W HEN I FIRST STARTED TEACHING children's literature, a
student brought in a copy of *The Happy Mother Goose*,
published around 1950. I grabbed it with delight, for rewritten versions of Mother Goose (and other classics) are a
hobby of mine — I love to collect bad examples — and
though I'd heard about this particular version I'd never
seen it. It did not let me down:

Three kind mice
Three kind mice

See how they run
See how they run
They all ran after the farmer's wife
Who cut them some cheese with a carving knife . . .

Doctor Foster went to Glou'ster
In a shower of rain.
He stepped in to a dry doorway
Till it was clear again.

There was a little girl and she had a little curl
Right in the middle of her forehead;
When she was good she was very, very good,
And never was naughty or horrid.

I took this book home and showed it to our girls, then about ten, eight, and six, and they read it through with mounting indignation and disgust.

"Who wants to read about standing in a doorway? What's the fun of *that?*"

"If Georgie Porgie doesn't kiss the girls and make them cry, what's the point of telling about him?"

They were particularly scathing about the little girl with the little curl. They hooted with derision. *Never* was naughty or horrid! What a lie! *Everybody* was naughty and horrid at some time or other.

My brother knew this, as all children do, at a very young age. Our favorite great-aunt, Aunt Ria, was visiting our grandparents. She seemed very old and spoke with a clipped British accent, since she'd been twelve when the family came over from Newcastle instead of six months, like my grandma. Craig had done something mildly naughty and Aunt Ria said to him, "Craig, why can't you be a *good* little boy?" Craig looked at her in solemn astonishment and replied, with his four-year-old lisp and in that deep voice he'd had since he was two — due to an accidental encounter with some cleaning compound from the milk house: "Aunt Wia — little boyths have to be *good* thome of the time and little boyths have to be *bad* thome of the time. I should think that you'd know that by *thith* time!"

In "I Didn't Mean to Be Bad" I talked about the times we wrongdo in innocence. Here, I'm talking about those times when we know full well that we're doing something naughty and horrid and we go right ahead and do it anyway, driven by who knows what meanness and spite and the desire to hurt someone else. This is an experience common to little boys and girls, also to big boys and girls, and, alas, to grown men and women.

Hopefully, as we grow older we learn better how to act toward other people so that they will in turn act better toward us. But it's pretty hard, when someone is mean to us, not to be mean back.

Examples from animals aren't usually valid for human emotions, but I can't resist directing you to the book *King Solomon's Ring*, by Konrad Lorenz, one of my heroes. He is an ethologist, one who studies animal behavior. He has a chapter on the pecking order in a colony of jackdaws. As a farm kid I knew about pecking order, and witnessed it in the chicken yard — there was always one chicken that every other chicken pecked, a poor bedraggled hen that scuttled around trying to be inconspicuous and keep away from all the other chickens. One who had lost most of her feathers, whose bare rear end and head were bloody masses.

Some other hens had the same trouble, but to a lesser degree. For there was a definite pecking order: at the top, a hen — or the rooster when there was one — who was able to peck every other fowl in the yard, yet none of them dared peck back. Second in line, the hen who could peck every other fowl except the top fowl, and so on down to the bottom of the pecking order, where resided the poor chicken that every other chicken could peck, but she couldn't peck any of the others. Hence her woeful state.

Well, Lorenz's jackdaw colony differed from the hen yard in that there were a great many male birds, and he discovered that the wife of a jackdaw, as is often the case in human society also, shared her husband's place in the social order. So there were two top birds, two next-to-top, unless a bird were unmarried in which case he occupied the spot alone, and so on, with the weak, young, and female singletons at the bottom. Lorenz's best story is about one of these miserable spinsters, who received every other bird's pecks and led a life of harassment. Oddly enough she attracted a bachelor jackdaw who was high on the pecking order. He took her as his mate, and immediately her social position shot nearly to the top. Overnight, she became able to peck all the birds below her, male and female. And because she had been on the bottom rung of the ladder, and knew what it was like to lead a life of misery, did she now show compassion to the less fortunate jackdaws beneath her? No. That is not bird nature. She became as vicious a pecker as any jackdaw in the colony.

Often we show bird nature, too. We're pecked, we peck back — if we can. If we can't, we peck someone below us in the line. We have an advantage over jackdaws in that we can peck back with more imagination, and if we're at the bottom of the line we may be clever enough to conceal our pecking back, and land a jab on somebody high up without his knowing where the peck is coming from — which saves our rump, and gives a wicked satisfaction. I was little and sneaky like that, for with older sisters I was definitely not King of the Roost.

"Badness," of course, has many interpretations. Is pecking back — revenge, getting even — bad? Maybe it depends on how it's done. Or how about the "badness" of Tom Sawyer and Huck Finn, or Thomas Bailey Aldrich in his *The Story of a Bad Boy:*

This is the story of a bad boy. Well, not such a very bad, but a pretty bad boy; and I ought to know, for I am, or rather I was, that boy myself.

Lest the title should mislead the reader, I hasten to assure him here that I have no dark confessions to make. I call my story the story of a bad boy, partly to distinguish myself from those faultless young gentlemen who generally figure in narratives of this kind, and partly because I really was *not* a cherub. I may truthfully say I was an amiable, impulsive lad, blessed with fine digestive powers, and no hypocrite. I didn't want to be an angel and with the angels stand. . . . I was a real human boy . . . and no more like the impossible boy in the story-book than a sound orange is like one that has been sucked dry.

This sort of badness is more a mischievous sort of naughtiness; boyhood pranks. (Have you ever heard of *girlhood* pranks? Neither have I.) These cause adults distress, but the deeds aren't malicious or done with an evil heart.

Speaking of Tom and Huck, Mark Twain has a short story about a gentleman who climbs into a railway carriage, which in England is like a little room with space for several people on each side facing each other, and finds himself with a woman and a lot of squirming children. He tells the children a story about a little boy who is so good that he keeps getting medal after medal for goodness. When the little boy and his bad little friends are out playing in a field, the wolf comes along. All the bad children scamper away but the good boy is so encumbered by his medals that he can't move fast enough and the wolf eats him up. Whereupon the gentleman tips his hat and steps out of the carriage, leaving gaping children and a scandalized mama. This story is more fun when you put it in historical perspective. When Mark Twain and Thomas Bailey Aldrich were writing, practically every story for children was about *good* little children, who never were naughty or horrid.

These stories were supposed to teach children to be good by good example, and to shun being bad by seeing that bad children came to dreadful ends. Mark Twain reversed this in his short story, which is a spoof, a satire, a parody of that kind of goody-goody literature.

Another writer who did it, thirty years later (about 1900), was Hilaire Belloc. In his *Cautionary Tales for Children* the hero of each tale is a "bad" child, but the badness is very minor or not bad at all. Yet it leads him, or her, to a more gruesome end than any of the stories Belloc is parodying. He spoofs by exaggeration:

> *The Chief Defect of Henry King*
> *Was chewing little bits of String,*

and these knotted in his insides and killed him. (Said the physicians, as they took their fees, "There is no Cure for this Disease.") Then there was Jim, who let go of his nurse's hand at the zoo and was eaten by a lion:

> *Now just imagine how it feels*
> *When first your toes and then your heels,*
> *And then by gradual degrees,*
> *Your shins and ankles, calves and knees,*
> *Are slowly eaten, bit by bit.*
> *No wonder Jim detested it!*

And Rebecca, who slammed doors and was killed by a marble statue that toppled from the wall above:

> *She was not really bad at heart,*
> *But only rather rude and wild:*
> *She was an aggravating child. . . .*

The German *Struwwelpeter* is a book so appalling that most kids delight in it. The great tailor, for instance, in his tight red trousers leaps across the page and cuts off the thumbs of "naughty little Suck-a-thumb," while his mama calmly says, "I knew he'd come."

You'll also enjoy an anthology our girls have read over and over, *Naughty Children*, where sometimes the naughtiness is innocent, sometimes deliberate. (An anthology takes bits and pieces out of all sorts of books, in case you didn't know, and leads you to a lot of good reading you might miss otherwise.) Then there's the book of poems, *Beastly Boys and Ghastly Girls*, edited by William Cole; and *My Naughty Little Sister* is now enchanting Elspeth. I just overheard, though, a comment by literary critic Jill, seconded by Megan: "We always liked what the *Naughty Little Sister* stories were *about*, but not the soupy way they were *written!*"

There is a vicarious delight in hearing about others doing wicked things you wouldn't dare to do, and getting punishments you don't have to suffer. In *Sister*, the writer is once removed by telling the stories about someone else. This is a good writing device, in spite of the soupy style — *you* would never have been that fractious! It's the Goops, not you, who always lick their fingers and lead outrageous lives.

As you can see, there's a rich literature of horridness, and I've barely scratched the surface. Badness makes very good reading, I guess because we can empathize so well.

A friend-of-friends used to tell stories about three sisters named Goodina, Terriblina, and In-Betweena. My friend's children weren't much interested in Goodina and In-Betweena, but they begged to hear the adventures of Terriblina! Our kids would much rather hear about the times they were bad than about when they were good. They especially like to hear about when their parents were bad, and grandparents too. It links up the generations in this fallen world. "Tell us about the time your mother was ready to back out and she said 'Is anything coming?' and none of you kids bothered to look and you all chorused 'no' and she backed right out into another car!"

I find it hard to remember the good stories — see the "Miseries" chapter — while the bad ones are still fresh in my memory. There's the time I threw my milk in my brother's face when he was being insufferable; I was about ten at the time — and then eight years later, when he was being insufferable again, and taunted me, "I suppose you're going to throw your milk again?" the same irresistible feelings surged up and I doused him a second time.

Laura Ingalls Wilder recounts her own naughtiness, complete with ugly thoughts and unhappy feelings. One passage where she's deliberately bad is in *On the Banks of Plum Creek*. Nellie, an offensive girl, comes to Laura's party. She tells Mrs. Ingalls she didn't wear her best dress just to come to a country party, and in various other ways makes herself unpleasant. Laura is furious, and devises a scheme to get even with Nellie. She steers her to the creek to wade, and then frightens her with tales of a big crab and sends her splashing upstream to wait in the still, deep, muddy water while Laura goes back and forth pretending to scare the nonexistent crab away. When Nellie returns to the clear water:

> Muddy-brown bloodsuckers were sticking to her legs and her feet. She couldn't wash them off. She tried to pick one off, and then she ran screaming up on the creek bank. There she stood kicking as hard as she could, first one foot and then the other, screaming all the time.
>
> Laura laughed till she fell on the grass and rolled. . . .
>
> "Laura!" Mary said. "You get up and pull those things off, or I'll tell Ma."
>
> Then Laura began to pull the bloodsuckers off Nellie. All the girls watched and screamed while she pulled them out long, and longer, and longer. Nellie cried: "I don't like your party!" she said. "I want to go home!" . . .

Laura did not care. . . . Deep down inside her Laura felt satisfied when she thought of Nellie dancing on the creek bank.

Sometimes our experience is that way. We never regret our evil deed. A certain fifth grader, who wrote in to WHA radio station in response to this subject, hasn't yet. He told of the time he got even with his sister. She was scared silly of snakes, and Richard happened to find a little grass snake one day while she was taking a bath. He guided it through the crack under the bathroom door, waited — and the results were spectacular:

She screamed and screamed and screamed. She didn't dare get out of the bathtub and unlock the door. My dad finally had to put up a ladder and rescue her through the window. I really got it, but boy, was it worth it!

Sometimes we enjoy our meanness at the time, but when we later realize how badly we've hurt someone, we wish we could go back and undo it. This happened to Caddie in *Caddie Woodlawn*, after she and her brothers played nasty pranks on their ladylike Boston cousin. And sometimes when we're doing horrid things, we feel horrid while we're doing them, but seem to be forced along by a will not our own.

Harriet, that rich book, comes up again. When Harriet writes in her notebook her honest thoughts about her friends, not all of what she writes is "good" in the sense that her friends will like what she's written. She loses her notebook and her friends read it. They're hurt and angry, and use various cruel methods of getting even. Harriet then is also hurt, angry — and alone.

SOMETHING IS DEFINITELY HAPPENING TO ME. I AM CHANGING. I DON'T LIKE ME AT ALL. I DON'T

EVER LAUGH OR THINK ANYTHING FUNNY. I JUST
FEEL MEAN ALL OVER. I WOULD LIKE TO HURT
EACH ONE OF THEM IN A SPECIAL WAY THAT
WOULD HURT ONLY THEM.

She makes a list:

MARION HAWTHORNE: FROGS. PUT ONE IN HER
DESK. A SNAKE WOULD BE BETTER.
RACHEL HENNESSEY: HER FATHER. ASK HER WHERE
HE WENT.
LAURA PETERS: HER HAIR. CUT IT OFF. OR MAKE A
BALD SPOT.
PINKY WHITEHEAD: MEAN LOOKS. THAT'S ALL HE
NEEDS.
CARRIE ANDREWS: TELL HER FATHER SOMETHING
TERRIBLE ABOUT HER WHICH IS A LIE. . . .

Later, at home, she still feels mean:

"I have a new cake in the oven," whispered the cook. "It
will be ready in a minute. You musn't bounce around, or
walk heavy, or shout, because it will fall."
Harriet stood there. She munched a thought over in her
mind. Without warning she ran to the center of the room,
overturned a chair, then jumped up and down, stomping her
feet with all her might. . . .

The story ends with Harriet in balance again, and she
and her friends made up. They've come through to a lot
more understanding. This is a book that tells you quite a
bit about the feeling of being horrid, what causes it, what
you can do about it, and so forth, which sounds preachy
here, but the book isn't. I recommend it.
And I'm also suggesting that *you* add to the literature of
beastliness. Try writing a cautionary tale à la Belloc. Try a

Ghastly Girl poem. Or *why* did that old woman spank all those children? Try a "naughty little sister." But most interesting of all will be the accounts of your own deliberate badness. These will not only make lively reading for yourself and your friends — and parents and future offspring, if you ever dare show them — but might help you to understand the happening better, to see what your own feelings were, and why. And to understand the other fellow.

What were your boyhood/girlhood pranks? Did any of these backfire, and turn out to be not funny? Even harmful? Did you do them as "innocently" as you thought, or were you fooling yourself?

When you were being horrid and knowing it, were you pecking because you'd been pecked? Put in the details! Think about what caused you to do what you did, not just the trigger cause but the underlying reasons, if you can figure them out. How you felt before you did the deed or said the words, and during, and afterwards. When did your feelings change? Did you feel triumph? Joy? Delight? Regret? Remorse? Guilt? Fear of retaliation? Fear of punishment? Self-pity? Mean all the time? Were you ever found out?

And what about "getting it"? Is it ever worth it? Do you *like* to be punished for a wrongdoing; does it clear the air? (You've heard an adult say about a small child, "He's aching for a spanking!") Or does it depend on the type of punishment, or whether it's fair or not, in proportion to the crime? We once found ourselves part of a spontaneous discussion on punishments, and the kids — not ours; they weren't born yet — generally felt that they preferred something quick and clean, like a swat, rather than having privileges taken away, or for adults to blanket them with blame and guilt or, worse, a heart-to-heart talk!

I think the problem with the last, and why it's unpopular, is that we are so unskilled in really talking to each other, communicating about things that matter, such as the depths of our horrid feelings — or our tender feelings.

And it's been my experience that once I write something out, I find it much easier to say these feelings, and a lot more besides, to the person to whom it really matters that I say them.

Such as to the person I've hurt. Or who has hurt me.

13

Mud Between Your Toes

"The corpse's teeth," whispered Janice in the dark, and fumbled into Marcy's hand several small, jagged pebbles. Marcy passed them on to Betsy.

"The corpse's tongue."

The part-firm, part-soft body of a clam, extracted from its shell.

"The corpse's skin."

Some of that ruffly rough seaweed that felt like crepe paper.

"The corpse's eyeball."

A damp, peeled grape.

"The corpse's left ear."

A small, slimy, snail-notched lily pad.

"The corpse's toenails."

Dried fish scales.

"The corpse's tonsils. Please handle with extreme care."

Thad had consented to having his pickled tonsils used in the Chamber of Horrors if they were treated with respect. Marcy shuddered as they came into her hands. They were round and wrinkly and rubbery, and smelled strongly of preservative. She wondered if there were any other people in the whole history of the world who had ever sat in the dark, passing pickled tonsils from hand to hand.

— From a radio version of *The Ghost Boat*

T HAT PASSAGE DESCRIBES a game generally used at Halloween for the parts of the witch, but here the kids are using it for their ghost, the corpse of the drowned fisherman. Those feels, of course, are intended to make your flesh prickle and your blood run chill. But there are many kinds of feels, from detestable to delectable.

Do you know why
I'm wearing shorts?

That's so I can feel
More of the skin.
— Sara, age 6,
about to have
her first
horseback ride

I have a lot of favorite feels. The spongy springiness of walking barefoot on a moss bed. The somewhat different feel of passing my hand gently over moss. Different mosses have different feels, and so does the same moss at different points of its growing cycle. Then I've always liked the strong sloppy suction of a calf sucking on my fingers, with his incredibly rough tongue. When I retrieve my tingling fingers I marvel that there's anything left of them, and have renewed respect for how the cow stands it so placidly.

Have you ever been licked by a cat? The tongue is delicate, refined, like a smooth grade of sandpaper, and barely wet. A dog, now, is very juicy when he kisses, and he covers a lot more area with considerably more vigor. When my aloof goat, Sugarpuss, would deign to notice me, she'd breathe gently all over my face, nibble on a wisp of my hair, and finish with a quick, sharp pull. All feels I liked.

At the school our older three attend is a snake, Ignatz, whose favorite spot is in someone's sleeve with the tip of his tail hanging out. The kids report that they like his clean, cool length along their arms, and I presume that Ignatz mutually enjoys their warm flesh or he wouldn't stay there.

Mud is another favorite feel of mine, walking through puddles or in thick squdgy mud that oozes up between my toes. I like e.e. cummings's description: When the world is "mud-luscious," and "puddle-wonderful." Sometimes, in a wet field, the mud will coat my feet into heavy boots, and the slogging along takes great effort. I like best a just-plowed field when the ground is moist and pungent (and the birds are going mad with the overturned worms), and as I walk my feet crumble the ridges into the furrows. But pure torture is the same field when the plowed clods have dried and hardened to jagged brick, and you must hobble across it on spring-tender feet!

And surely you've made mudpies. Mixing the dirt to just the right consistency. Rolling the dough into snakes, balls, twists. Pounding it into pancakes. Wasn't it perfect pleasure? The delights of mud are pretty universal, I'd guess, except for those deprived people who have been overtrained to be overclean, and think that dirt is evil. I have a Little Golden Book called *My Baby Brother*, where the big sister says, "My baby brother likes to play in the mud. That is naughty. I have to scold him." And she'll grow up to be a mother!

Have you ever noticed how two sensations can be alike and yet the effect on you is very different? One of Elspeth's favorite feels is the tickle of a ladybug walking up her arm. A spider makes much the same tickle, but most people would react to the spider with revulsion. A friend of ours after twenty years still examines his pajamas before he puts them on, because he once discovered a spider in the bottoms.

Touching, feeling, is the other neglected sense of our major five, along with taste and smell. It shouldn't be. But our culture puts a lot of taboos on touching. We're taught, "Don't touch," "Keep your hands off" — off of things, and especially people. We get the understanding early in our lives that it's not quite nice to touch, or to enjoy the sensation of feeling. I know grade schools and high schools where it's even written into the contract that a teacher must never touch a child in any way. This cuts out physical punishment but it also does away with an encouraging pat on the back, or an arm around the shoulder.

This attitude toward touch bothered me when Elspeth was in nursery school and I was there on my days as mother-helper. There was an elfin girl, Natasha, from Germany, all huge bright eyes and shy smile. She didn't speak a word of English. But she would sidle up to a boy on the rug, during story time, and put her arms around him, or would stroke the long hair of the girl in front of her. She would hug and kiss on the playground, gently, not aggressively. Most of the children didn't seem to mind Natasha's affections, but they were of constant concern to the teachers.

"Don't touch, Natasha!" "Keep your hands to yourself, Natasha!" "Sit over by yourself, Natasha!" They would lift her hand in mid-stroke from Kelly's golden hair and lay it firmly in her lap with a reprimanding pat. So Natasha was learning, as were the other kids, that there's something wrong with touching, with expressing your pleasure in long silky hair by stroking it. And for her, this must've been especially frustrating. She couldn't communicate by talking to the others, or understand their speech. Her language was her own little, loving body, and she was forbidden to use it.

I think people fear touch because it's such a personal thing; it's closer than hearing or seeing, where you can keep more distance. Touch comes direct to our skin, be it by wind or by fingers, and no sense is more "physical," though perhaps taste, also rather taboo, is its equal there. And a lot of people are afraid of their bodies. They're afraid because they're men or women or boys or girls, afraid because they are sexual creatures. And so these touching taboos continue.

Yet touching, feeling, using our skin to give and receive messages, is an important way we learn — look at how babies feel and taste everything — and is an essential part of being human. I've already quoted the place where Tolly, in *Treasure of Green Knowe,* learns how intelligent his feet are: how they can feel and understand, even through shoes. From the same book, here are descriptions of blind Susan's need to touch. Tolly says, "I don't like being touched by things I can't see," and his grandmother replies,

"That's one of the disadvantages of having eyes. They make people afraid when they can't see. Everything that Susan touched was something she couldn't see. But far from being afraid, she wanted to catch everything in the act of being real. She even put her finger in the candle flame to see what being burned was like."

The description of Susan continues:

. . . it was dreadful never to be allowed to try to do anything herself. She was an active, intelligent little person full of curiosity. She wanted to crawl, to walk, to explore, to find out where people vanished to, to touch and handle everything and learn what things were and where they could be found again.

Nanny Softly [was a] kind stupid woman, and wouldn't let her alone. Let Nanny do it, Nanny will fetch it, Nanny will button it, Nanny will tie it, Nanny will feed you, Nanny will wash your hands. Anything Susan wanted to try for herself she had to do quickly while Nanny wasn't there. Once Nanny caught her warming her own hands by the fire, and once actually standing at the top of the stairs, and she let out a scream that Susan would fall and kill herself and carried her away and strapped her in a chair. After that she lived strapped in a chair, except when she sat a prisoner on Nanny's knee, or somebody led her by the hand. In leading her, they were impatient, because their idea was to get her quickly where they were going, while Susan's idea was to feel everything possible on the way there. Everything was to her most mysterious, because she only felt a bit of it as she was dragged past, a ledge or a knob, a fold of curtain, or perhaps she felt nothing, but there was a different smell or a hollower sound. She had no idea how big things were or what shape. They stuck out of space like icebergs out of the sea. For this reason she enjoyed the continuous pleasantly shaped stair rail and liked to draw her fingers along the banisters as she went up and down, pushed and pulled by Nanny Softly. . . .

Very soon Susan began to resent Nanny, who fussed her and thwarted her and captured her hands and held them while the cup was put to her lips, because she might spill it, and wiped her mouth for her, and slapped her hands when they fingered things of great interest, such as frills being ironed. There were battles and tempers, and the punishment was to be strapped in her chair again and left there. . . .

She was allowed to let the string of pearls run through her fingers or the diamonds lie in her palm. She loved the pearls, and anything like filigree or twisted gold chains or lockets on velvet ribbon or rings; but she could not imagine why diamonds were so precious. They were hard, heavy, edgy, and cold. . . . Maria never let Susan wear any of the jewels herself, beyond slipping her little hand through a bracelet, and that was soon taken away lest she should drop it. Neither Maria nor Mrs. Softly seemed to realize that Susan never dropped anything. . . .

"You can take Susan. I've had enough of her for tonight." Susan would hardly be allowed to press the clasp of a lid together before she was hauled away, leaving behind her all the fascinating leather boxes, oval, or oblong, or domed to take a high bracelet, each box scented and lined in silk or velvet, with a notch that exactly fitted what was to lie there and a satisfactory snap when the lid was closed. It was like being dragged from heaven. Her lingering fingers pinched the lace ruffles round the dressing table, but Nanny Softly was relentless.

"Come along now, Miss Susan. How often have I told you fingering is bad manners."

Another of our favorite books is *A High Wind in Jamaica*, by Richard Hughes, where a group of children get carried away on a pirate ship. It contains a tremendous lot of interesting "touch" sensations, of which these are only a few:

In the shallows the small ones rolled and chuckled. Emily, for coolness, sat up to her chin in water, and hundreds of infant fish were tickling with their inquisitive mouths every inch of her body, a sort of expressionless light kissing. Anyhow she had lately come to hate being touched — but this was abominable. At last, when she could stand it no longer, she clambered out and dressed.

"Harold has brought his alligator," said Rachel.

Harold stepped forward, and laid the little creature on Emily's coverlet. It was very small: only six inches long: a yearling: but an exact miniature of its adult self. . . . Emily was translated into Heaven. So this was an alligator! She was actually going to sleep with an alligator! . . . Emily lifted a finger and began to rub the corner of his jaw. The hiss changed to a sound almost like a purr. A thin, filmy lid first covered his eye from the front backwards, then the outer lid closed up from below.

Suddenly he opened his eyes again, and snapped on her finger: then turned and wormed his way into the neck of her nightgown, and crawled down inside, cool and rough against her skin, till he found a place to rest. It is surprising that she could stand it, as she did, without flinching.

Pigs grow quickly, quicker even than children. . . . He soon grew to such a size one could not possibly allow him to lie on one's stomach anymore: so, as his friendliness did not diminish, the functions were reversed, and it became a common thing to find one child, or a whole bench of them, sitting on his scaly side. . . . One cannot wish for a more comfortable seat than an acquiescent pig.

"If I was the Queen," said Emily, "I should most certainly
have a pig for a throne."

"Perhaps she has," suggested Harry.

"He *does* like being scratched," she added presently in a
very sentimental tone, as she rubbed his scurfy back. . . .

"I don't think I should kiss him quite so much if I was
you," Emily presently advised Laura, who was lying with
her arms tight around his neck and covering his briny snout
with kisses from ring to ears.

There's also *The Wind in the Willows*, filled with touch,
and in *Charlotte's Web*, Wilbur at one point enjoys a but-
termilk bath, and at night in the barn pushes aside the
scratchy straw to stretch out in the delightfully soft cow
manure.

And for pure hilarity, nothing can beat Mark Twain's
Connecticut Yankee in King Arthur's Court, where the
Yankee, riding on his quest, encounters heat, sweat, itchi-
ness, and a fly inside his armor.

We can't all get kissed by fish, sleep with an alligator,
sit on a pig, roll in manure, but we can certainly extend our
range of feel experiences by becoming more aware of the
nuances of the feels we already know, their fine shades of
difference; and also by consciously seeking and appreciat-
ing new feels.

Maria Montessori, the Italian educator of seventy-five
years ago, trained her schoolchildren to be very discrimi-
nating in touch. Perhaps she was the inspiration for my
friend Louisa Liske's *Touching Book*. Louisa has stapled a
variety of materials together, and her kindergartners like to
sit and feel the velvet and silk and nylon and felt and tweed
and dotted swiss. They get to be quite touch-discerning.
She also has a whole booklet of sandpaper for them, from
the very finest to the heavy rough stuff coated with actual
pebbles, and a tray full of "feeling pieces." This contains
wave-polished stones, chestnut burrs, black walnut shells,

clinging weed pods, all sorts of interesting feels, and the children lend their own favorite pocket-pieces to the collection. You could play a game with these, like the Chamber of Horrors, passing them from hand to hand to see how skillful you are at identifying them, and also taking the opportunity to enjoy the touch sensations. We've done this, hiding each "feelie" in a numbered paper bag. Do different stones have different feels? Why is soapstone named as it is? Do all barks feel alike? And what's that awful slimy touch? A banana skin?

How about people skin? Compare the front of your elbow with your alligator skin on the back; your palm with the back of your hand; the peculiar convolutions and ridges and textures of the inside of your ear — as interesting to touch as to draw — with your little soft and waggly ear lobe. Touch a very old person's skin, and a baby's.

Try sculpting in clay with your eyes shut, so that you're guided only by your sense of feel. Make things that are supposed to be touched; have a Touch Me exhibit. And try again the activities in the "Blind" chapter, concentrating on your sense of touch.

The more experience you have with feels, as with any sense, the richer you are. The more that you share your experiences vividly in your writing — the rubbery tonsils as well as the delicate dandelion puff — the more alive your writing will be, and the more the reader will recognize (even feel, in his mind's touch) the same sensation you are describing. Then he's the richer, too. Trying to describe your sensations will also increase your own acuteness and ability to feel. Listing favorite ones, as I did with mine at the start of this chapter, is a good place to begin:

I Like to Feel
the tiny prickle of a warm rain
a buffeting wind that you can actually lean into
the fuzzy head of a new baby

Uggy Feels
seaweed brushing my foot when I'm swimming
stepping on a dog poop
the catch in my side from running
the itch I can't scratch

Then go on to tell in more detail what these feels are like.
Avoid the stereotypes that no longer have meaning because
they are so common: soft as silk, hard as a rock.

You might recall incidents that involved touching and
feeling, such as the Natasha story, and write them down
with as much detail as you can. I remember the time my
sister, for a joke, tried to wake me up one morning by putting perfume under my nose. Have you ever awakened
your dog by holding a bit of hamburger in front of his
nostrils and watched him go through who knows what delicious dreams, accompanied by snorts and twitchings, till
he suddenly woke up and snatched the morsel? That's
being awakened by *smell*, and Patty intended to wake me
that way with the strong perfume. Did she expect me to
twitch, to smile? If so, she should have just held the bottle
under my nose. Instead she put the perfume on my upper
lip, and I woke with a start because the touch of the liquid
was *cold*. The feel beat out the smell.

Pat also used to give me "sweat baths." We shared a bedroom and sometimes she would rip the covers off her bed
and pounce with them on me, keeping me prisoner in the
hot cocoon of my own bed. The more I'd struggle to get
free of the mountains of blankets, the redder and sweatier
I would get, and the more beneficial the sweat bath would
be to me — or so she said.

I've also never forgotten the chicken legs. When Bob and
I were in England a couple years after we were married, we
were visiting an elderly couple on a farm in the Cotswolds.
At dusk Basil discovered that all his chickens had gotten

loose and were roosting on the low branches of the trees near the hen yard. He wanted those hens safely back in the coop before dark so they'd not come to harm in the night, and called us to help. He went around rather testily plucking them out of trees as though he were picking flowers, except that once he had a chicken picked he put her in the other hand upside down so that it was like holding a bouquet of roses — or rather, white peonies — wrong-way-to. After he'd collected four or five he suddenly thrust the bouquet at me and said, "Here, put these in the hen house." I grabbed that bunch of chicken legs and received a real shock: *the legs were warm.* In spite of being a farm girl I'd never felt live chicken legs, and unconsciously expected something cold, as from the refrigerator, even though common sense would have told me that of course hens are warm-blooded, of course their legs will be warm. The legs were also smooth and scaly, but that was a minor touch sensation compared to the temperature.

Our blind friend Edie told us a person-touching story and I admire the seventh-grade boy who prompted it: Edie'd been in "seeing" school for several weeks when one day the boy who sat across from her in English left his chair, touched her, and returned to his seat. That's all. Just touched her. She turned and smiled toward him. I think he wanted to make her *real* to him, and him to her, as blind Susan wanted to make things real. And he chose touch, not speech, as the means of doing it.

We all need to touch, and not just things. We need it as much at ten and older as we did when we were small. So let's not neglect it or feel uncomfortable or embarrassed that we enjoy it. We love to snuggle babies, and if babies don't get cuddling they grow up stunted emotionally — or curl up and die. All of us don't have babies around to hug, but there are other creatures that will serve, and that are delighted to be touched themselves. Cats rub against us.

Dogs beg for a pat. A frog will sit still indefinitely if you stroke him gently between the eyes. You can even tickle fish; it's called guddling.

And have you noticed that grandparents can manage quite a big child in their laps? Grandparents need hugging, need touchable companionship, just as much as you do. I might venture to add, so do poor old parents.

14

How (Maybe) to Write a Book

A T MY FIRST CIRCUIT of the book fairs a few years ago, I listened to the other authors speak, and realized after a bit that all of them were giving one of three talks:

1. They talked about their book just published; why they wrote it, the research they did for it, the story of it, etc.

2. They tried to get the audience to talk. They asked the kids questions, mainly: what do you like to read, and why?

3. Or, they talked about How to Write a Book.

And every time I heard that last talk, it was the same flavor of Jell-O. Only one talk would have bananas and another, fruit salad.

The first time, in Chicago, I thought, "Oh well, that's only one man's opinion." The next day I heard it in Cleveland, from a woman, and by the time I heard it again, in Columbus, I was really puzzled, and rather disturbed, for the way these three authors said was How to Write a Book wasn't at all the way I'd ever written one (except once; I'll tell you later) or that I'd advise anybody to, especially kids.

The Columbus speaker was quite a well-known and successful children's author. I think he's one of the few who make a living at it. He stood up in front of an auditorium full of eager schoolchildren, and told them that first you decide on your idea, what you want your book to be about. Then you pick out your characters, who will be in the book. You list them, and under each name you fill in everything about them. So-and-so is blue-eyed and skinny and has warts, he tells silly jokes, teases his sister, and raises guppies. With everything down, you won't make mistakes as you write and give him brown eyes in one chapter.

Then — or maybe sort of at the same time — you figure out your plot, what's going to happen to your character. You do this plotting bit with an outline, you know, the I, A, 1, a stuff. And you have to be sure to get the details right, Author X said. For instance, if your story is set in 1812 and calls for a carriage, you'd better check out whether an 1812 carriage had springs or not, for that'll make a difference when you describe a carriage ride. You'll bump a lot or not so much.

And finally, when you get your outline all finished and your characters all figured out and the details all in, then you're ready to go. Then you can actually begin to *write* your story.

The Cleveland author wrote her books this way, too, and

she told about a writing team she knew, a husband and wife, who put their outline on the dining room wall. When, after weeks of planning and plotting they had filled up the entire wall with the details of their book-to-be, "they knew it was time to start to write."

To return to the Columbus author, he described the actual writing in this way: "It's just something you have to do. Like sitting down to do your homework, or practicing the piano, instead of being outside playing baseball." (No conception, you notice, that somebody might *like* to do some homework, might *like* to practice the piano.) It's drudgery, his whole attitude was, and if you're going to write a book it just has to be gotten over with, plowed through, no matter how distasteful it is. This takes another long time. Then, when you've fleshed out the bare bones of your outline and have your first draft, you take it and go over it all again. And again. And again. And *again*, until you're satisfied that it's done. Then, all neatly typed, it goes off to the publisher and if it's accepted you have the chore of going over it yet again, after the copy editor has made all his changes and corrections, and next it gets set in print, on long sheets of paper called galley proofs, and you have to go over it once more to be sure there aren't any errors in the type, and finally it gets printed up in finished form and the hard covers put on and it's out in the book stores, ready to buy, and that's how to write a book. Any questions?

All this he said at much more length than I have given it, and in a pretty monotonous tone, while the audience gradually sank deeper in their seats in a kind of stupor. Eventually a boy near the front raised his hand. The author motioned to him, the boy stood up — limply, his shoulders sagging. "Mr. X," he said wearily, "do you really think it's worth it?"

In the back of the room, hidden by the crowd, I burst

into wild applause and everybody joined in, laughing and clapping. For it was so exactly the question he deserved.

The day before, the Cleveland author had quoted Robert Louis Stevenson, "I don't like to write but I like having written," with that same idea — what awful dullness it is to write a book — "but it's so nice to have done it after it's over!"

Another author visiting at Columbus had given a lively talk on his latest book, and though I had never read any of his stuff or even heard of him till that day, he was a dynamic sort of fellow who, when I'd earlier walked into the authors' lounge from the airport, boomed out before he'd even met me, "Thank God for a pretty dress! Most of these authors don't care whether they give the kids anything nice to look at or not!" So of course I was strongly disposed to approve of everything about *him*. I thought his books certainly ought to have more spirit than Author X's, and also his views on book writing to veer from the party line.

I caught him as he was leaving the building to rush to a TV interview.

"Mr. Y," I called, "do you outline your stories?"

"Of course," he bellowed, going out the door.

I followed him as he climbed into a taxi. "*Why* do you outline your stories?"

He rolled down a window. "Because if I didn't I wouldn't know where I was going!"

"Why do you *have* to know where you are going?" I shouted, but the taxi had whisked him away and I never saw him again. (Actually I did, the next year, but it makes a better story this way.)

Why do you have to know where you're going? I studied with a teacher of writing in graduate school, Roy Cowden at the University of Michigan, and he once said, "Writing is like climbing a mountain. You see the peak up there, and you climb up, going this way and that through the forest, and when you get to the top you look around and discover that you're only on a foothill." The real story you're telling is over there — and so you go on, and climb to the next peak, and maybe that's it, or maybe it's yet another foothill. Not that the foothills aren't worthwhile. All the time there is the pleasure and the exertion of climbing, and it's necessary to get to the top in order to see if there is another peak. You're also developing your mountain legs. The exploration along the way is rewarding, and there is the tang of the mystery: you know you don't know what lies beyond the peak you can see. You're the one who will find out, and you have the thrill of the discoverer.

The problem with those authors who tell How to Write a Book, it seems to me, is that they are figuring out their books from the bottom of the mountain, charting every detail of their way, and then when they begin to climb — to fill in the outline — they are so bounded by their map that they don't see the fork in the trail, they don't decide suddenly to leave the path and strike out through the brush or over the cliffs, or to follow a deer — and when they get to the peak, the one they saw from the bottom, they have such blinders on that they don't look around and realize they're only on a foothill. They say, "Aha, I'm here," and plunk down and take off their shoes. No wonder they don't have any fun, they only like "having written."

For me, there has always been joy in the actual writing. Blank paper always made me itch — and still does — to fill it up with words, with pictures, to create a story. I'm sure a beautiful empty notebook was the reason I wrote my first book. It was begging for filling. So on the first page I wrote in a poem I'd made up in second grade, the year before:

Five white ducks
Went down to the pond to swim.

149

There they found a nice old log.
From that they did jump in.
They paddled till they came to shore,
Ruffled their feathers and went back for more.

But the second page was blank, so I wrote a story on that, five or six lines long, and that left the third page. I decided to write a whole book of poems and stories, to surprise my parents, who were away on a month's trip. My little brother decided that for his surprise he'd get over his lisp. He did, and I did. Our parents were delighted with both our surprises, and I entered my book in the city-wide Hobby Show in the YMCA gym. Among all the painted vases and stamp collections and wood carvings and oil paintings and matchbook collections, there it sat, with a blue ribbon on it — the only *book* anybody, young or old, in the whole city had entered. (It *is* nice to have written.)

So in the fourth grade I wrote another book, still short stories but I called them chapters, for each one was about the same characters, dog brothers named Bumpy and Billy Bones, and they did all the things I'd have liked to have done: build a tree house, float down the creek on a raft, build a soap box auto and enter it in the Soap Box Derby.

That got a first prize in the Hobby Show, too — and was again the only book entered. I saw I had clear sailing in an uncontested sea.

My fifth-grade book was a much longer, continued story about a boy named Frenchy and a girl named Orania Turquoise, Turky for short, who go up in the clouds and visit the Oz-like countries on them. The *Cloudlanders* was seen and liked by a friend of my mother's, Mary Creighton, who was editor of a weekly newspaper down in Galesburg, Illinois. She printed it serially, and this was my first experience with how the printed word gobbles up the written. The story wasn't finished when it began to be published, and after it had run some months an issue came with no story, but with a box on the front page, saying:

> ATTENTION JACKIE DOUGAN:
> Authors shouldn't let their publishers get ahead of them. Send in the next installment pronto!

I was just leaving with my grandparents, the lucky child selected to go on a trip to visit relatives in Iowa, and that night, in a small hotel on the bluffs of the Mississippi, they went to bed while I sat up and wrote the next chapter on hotel stationery at a rickety little desk. Turky and Frenchy came rapidly down out of the clouds, after that.

With all this early success — and I haven't even mentioned *Maggie the Maggot* — you'd expect me to go on and tell you about my sixth-grade book, my seventh-grade book, and so forth. But after sixth grade I quit writing, except for a scattered piece or two, till I got to college. Why? Because of How to Write a Book. Or really, How to Write.

For we began in school about that time to learn to write properly. Maybe my teachers were only telling me how to write an essay, a research paper, what's known as "expository" writing rather than "creative" writing. *Coal Mining in Pennsylvania*. I can see, with a subject like that, the wisdom of reading up on coal mining, gathering data, figuring out how to organize it, trying various approaches, and finally, with a good outline, writing it. But I suspect my teachers and most teachers in general didn't make any distinction in kinds of writing, or didn't even think about books and stories — who wrote them? — for look at all those book-fair authors my age, give and take five or ten years, who thought coal-mining was the only way to write a book.

My own children have gotten this approach, too, and specifically in "creative" writing. They had a teacher who had her classes write books, and illustrate and bind them. But she had the kids work out their stories by plotting and outlines, so that they wouldn't end up with all sorts of unfocused material that didn't go anywhere. All right. You avoid that problem, but then you get into others that are more serious, I think. She also said that her purpose in having them do the book was for what they'd learn about composition, grammar, spelling, and so forth, and that goes along with the outlining. I think it's putting the cart before the horse, using the writing as a means to an end, rather than the writing itself being the higher goal.

So, when I was middle-school age, I didn't question my teachers, but began carefully to outline everything. Coal mining and cloudlanders. All my ideas for new books. I still have those outlines, in a briefcase I got for Christmas in third grade, where I kept all my writing. It also contains the beginnings of those outlined books, but no middles or endings.

The outlining, you see, soaked up all the creative surge. I'd get a good idea! I'd dash to write it down! But instead of starting the actual story, the first paragraph, I'd start an outline. Midway through it, the original impulse would dwindle away, for it was only a beginning idea, or a glimpse of the whole, without all the supporting details. A seed. And then there'd be nothing behind it to give it a shove — no weight (or fun) of the story already written to push it on to where to go next.

I asked a boy when I was once giving a book-fair talk, "Why do you read a book?"

"To find out what happens," he answered.

"That's why I write one," I said, and he was astonished. You'd think if anybody knew what was going to happen, the author would.

Well, some authors don't. For how do you know what your characters are like until you put them into a story and see how they act? Till then they're just paper dolls. How do you know what they'll turn into when the going gets rough? What other characters will unexpectedly emerge? When do you have the time to get to know them? An outline and a list of character traits won't do it. You have to live with them, move them here and there, and pretty soon they begin moving you. Your story and your characters run away with you and turn corners. Often you have to go back to the early part and change it, for something you made your hero do, back when you didn't know him so well, isn't what he would have done at all, you see now that you know him better. The writing is alive, right from the start, for the initial impulse is alive, and by the time that impulse is spent, like the initial stage of a rocket, your story has begun to take on a life of its own, burning its own fuel.

That's the real joy of writing — the life that's in it, the creating you're doing. As in real life you don't know what's going to happen next, or everything about the people you live with. They surprise you. You may have a pretty good idea — my story's going to go this direction, just as I'm going to get up and go to school tomorrow — but something could happen any minute to change that. I'd occasionally wake up to hear my father saying, downstairs, "I think I'll take Jackie with me today, for company, to that dairy parts factory in Kenosha," or "up to the experimental fields at the University," and then I'd hop out of bed and into my blue jeans rather than my school clothes.

For me, knowing what you're going to say before you say it takes away the vitality and makes the writing dreary.

Then it *is* just filling out the bare bones and it isn't worth it. Simply to have written isn't enough for me, and I'll bet it wasn't for Robert Louis Stevenson, either.

So, don't I plan a story at all? Sure, but I keep it in my mind as much as I can, where a new and better idea can knock it like a billiard ball and send it spinning to a pocket where it can be retrieved and used later, if I want to. Or I jot down a plan, not on a dining room wall, but on the back of an envelope and not a legal-size one, either. Also, I don't let the plans get too far ahead of where I am in the actual writing. I deliberately keep them vague.

I sometimes compare writing to going out to the barn on a dark night. You know the general direction of the barn, but the lantern only sheds direct light on the grass and pebbles a little way around you as you move. But if you change your mind, or go too far to the left, or aren't concentrating on the barn, you may end up at the corncrib instead. Once there it may be just where you really wanted to go, or, if it isn't, a useful detour, and you head for the barn again. In *Spruce Gum* I knew I wanted Libby to end up in harmony with her stepfather, but at the start, and even at the middle, I didn't know how I was going to get her there. The same in *Palefaces;* I wanted my kids to come to some sort of creative cooperation with the Boy Scouts, but I didn't know the steps. Writing it, one step just led to another, and if I made a false step, then I'd realize it after a while and back up — or jump over to the main track. However, either story *might* have led to a different ending.

The book I did write by outline was *Missing Melinda.* Our girls were bringing home stacks of mystery books, anything with "secret" or "hidden" or "mysterious" in the title, no matter how crummy, and I thought, I'd better write a mystery book; that'll make a lot of money, and then I can hire a baby-sitter once in a while and somebody to clean my filthy house, and carve out a little time to write what I really want to, which at that time was *Spruce Gum,* hardly off the ground. I asked the girls what they wanted, if I wrote a mystery, and they said twins and dolls; then I figured I *had* to have an outline, for with a mystery you do need to know where you're going, in order to plant the clues and have the right person caught at the end. So I wrote a chapter or two, to get in the spirit, and then in cold blood figured out the whole plot, who everybody was, what they did, and how it all came out, so that all the pieces fit together in good mystery-puzzle fashion. It was sort of fun, and I sold the chapters and outline to a publisher. I figured if the book turned out to be no good I could use a pseudonym — a false name — and nobody would know it was me.

But then came the time (after *Spruce Gum*, ironically, which had hotted up and gotten written in spite of no money) to write the story. To fill in the bones. I tried to do it and was bored stupid. It was tedious. I couldn't change the outline because it was committed the way it was. So I cast about for something to make it interesting enough to hold my attention, and decided to have the father a Shakespeare nut and to let the twins take turns writing the story, so that each chapter would be as if by one of them. This way Ophelia could comment on her sister's actions, ideas, appearance, and writing ability (and her own) as well as tell the story, and then Cordelia could have her cracks. This added the necessary fun and challenge to the writing, and the story turned out much the better on account of the changes. I was pleased to sign my own name to it. But it drove home my feeling that over-detailed planning can stunt creativeness.

Mr. Cowden told me another thing I've never forgotten: *get it down*. When you have a good idea, start writing. Keep on, and don't quit till you have down everything connected with that idea, it's all used up. Don't worry if it's good, bad, doesn't fit, is too long, too short, or anything. Just keep on getting it down. Don't go back and rewrite or polish, either. When you're fishing, you don't stop to clean a fish as soon as you catch it. You keep throwing in your line as fast as you can while the fish are biting. If you come to a hard spot you can't figure out, but the idea's still there ahead of you, solid ground beyond the pig wallow, leap and go on. When all the creative energy's used up you can go back and rewrite and polish to your heart's content, fill in the gaps, clean the fish. (That 1812 coach may go, entirely, and you never needed to look up about the springs at all.) What you've already written will spark new energy. But you won't have any left, if you spend it all on being fussy about a first paragraph, or a first chapter. So get it down.

Nobody can tell you how to write a story or a book. Those authors should have said, "How *I* Write a Book," and at least not saddled all of us with their method. I've said a lot here about how I, Jacqueline Jackson, write a book, but I also realize, aside from some general principles, that I've written all my books in different ways, grabbed them at different places. I could write a chapter on the writing of each book.

I've written them by getting the idea for the ending first, and writing that, and then going back and filling in the beginning and middle. Of course, when I got to the ending a second time I had to change it somewhat because of what had gone before, but there wouldn't ever have been that particular story if the ending hadn't come first. I've started one story and then switched in midstream, selecting one little idea out of it that suddenly grew big and needed a story all to itself. Even when I finish a story written neatly in order, the early part will have to have changes, because of the growth and the ending.

That's what rewriting's all about, and that has its own sorts of joys which I'll put in another chapter and call "How (Maybe) to Rewrite a Book."

15

Warty Bliggins, Smudley Croak: The Effanineffable Name

> What lovely names for girls there are!
> There's Stella like the Evening Star,
> And Sylvia like a rustling tree,
> And Lola like a melody,
> And Flora like a flowery morn,
> And Sheila like a field of corn,
> And Melusina like the moan
> Of water. And there's Joan, like Joan.
>
> What splendid names for boys there are!
> There's Carol like a rolling car,
> And Martin like a flying bird,
> And Adam like the Lord's First Word,
> And Raymond like the Harvest Moon,
> And Peter like a piper's tune,
> And Alan like the flowing on
> Of water. And there's John, like John.
>
> — "Girls' Names" and "Boys' Names,"
>   by Eleanor Farjeon

ONE THING THAT'S FUN about writing stories is that it gives you such a God-like power to name: people, animals, places, and even the title of the story or book itself. Or the power is maybe more Adam-like, since in Genesis God left the naming to Adam. I can picture Him saying, "Now look, Adam, I've worked hard all week and I'm bone-weary. You can just name all these creatures for me, can't you? Really a minor job . . ." and the spectacle of Every Living Thing (there are twenty thousand varieties of insects alone) lined up waiting to find out what they are, and Adam sitting there on a rock, his brow furrowed, chewing his pencil, scraping the bottom of the name barrel: "Walloby . . . aardvark . . . orangutan . . . ichneumon fly . . ."

My sisters, brother, and I, as farm denizens, were blessed with an almost Genesis-like quantity of animals to name. There were, for instance, a hundred cows, although we never gave a cow a personal name except when she dramatically distinguished herself from the herd either by looks or personality. My father had to name them all, however, for his records, and his solution to identification and bookkeeping was to give each bovine a letter, signifying the year she joined the herd, and then a number, showing her place in that year's sequence: J-11; G-16. But numbers weren't allowed when he registered his cows; they had to have names, so he translated the numbers into French, added "de Chez Nous" ("of our home"), and presto! the elegant name "M Treize de Chez Nous" for lowly M-13.

We did name all the batches of kittens that we regularly found, either close-eyed and mewing, or older and spitting, out in the hay. My mother was active in the National Federation of Music Clubs, and her mail held a variety of intriguing names on return addresses. These caught our fancy and during one season we named kittens after Mother's friends. This was okay when we called them Sadie and Maudie, and the kittens were little and cute. But to one black kitten we gave the whole euphonious name of Fernwood Scrimshaw, shortened to Fernwood, and that kitten became a large black cat who contracted a mangy disease on her neck. Daddy applied ointments and pills for weeks and Fernwood recovered, but the hair the length of her long neck never returned. Mother lived in dread that Mrs. Scrimshaw might some day show up at the farm and hear that denuded, scrawny cat being summoned, "Here Fernwood! Here Fernwood!"

We also named pet calves, a lamb, a couple of horses, a pair of pigs (Sausage and Petunia), my goats (Butter, Sugarpuss, Skyrocket, and Firecracker — the last two born on the Fourth of July), pet raccoons (Sig, Bundle), a pet squirrel (Andrew), a pet crow, and various dogs, most of whom, no matter what their real names, we called Boxer.

In addition we had our own pseudonyms. My pen name was P. Phineas Quigley, which I still sometimes use for fun, and I fought with my sister Patsy about my movie star name. I was going to be Zwiza Zwiza Zah, but Pat felt the last name should be Zwah, and she would declaim the whole name with great drama, mouthing out that last w. I insisted three zw's were too many, that a person needed the contrast of the stark "Zah" to go with the double Zwizas, and I still think so.

Most of us, however, don't have unlimited cows or kittens, so if the naming urge is strong in you, stories are an opportunity. I picked up off Jill's floor a couple of years ago,

> Some day, when everything costs nothing, and you pickle pickles to get cucumbers, I'm going to perform gallant deeds for gents in distress. Because when I get that old it's gents that are in distress and knightresses who save them. My name is March. I am twelve and the third eldest daughter. I have eleven sisters whose names are, from eldest to youngest, January, February, April, May, June, July, August, September, October, November, and December. I have seven brothers. . . .

When Demi was seven or eight she signed all her papers "Rebecca Twinkle," and when she was about ten I came across:

THE AZALIA FAMILY

Twin babies: Ivis Azalia
Avocet Azalia
Little girl: Gentian Azalia
Little Boy: Camas Azalia
Big Boys: Eider and Condor Azalia

In stories you don't have to use names you particularly like, of course. It's more important to pick the appropriate name, the name that sounds right and fits the character, whether it's Scrooge or Uriah Heep, Mr. Worldly-Wise or Pippilotta Provisionia Gaberdina Dandeliona Ephraimsdaughter Longstocking. I can remember my brother's delight, when he was reading about Archy the cockroach and Mehitabel the cat — pretty good names! — and came on the toad, Warty Bliggins. "What an absolutely perfect name for a toad!" he chortled, and we agreed. I bet Robert Frost chortled a little, too, as he wrote a poem about ants, and, needing a word to rhyme with formic, the acid in the little creatures, he came up with a worker ant named Jerry McCormic. Jill's been our Frost lover since first grade, and she gave a passing literature student hysterics when, at ten, she suddenly dropped to the sidewalk and exclaimed over a curled-up speck, "*Death's come to Jerry McCormic!*"

I find the name "Smudley Croak" in my notes. Scribbled on a piece of paper, no other identification. Where did it come from? Whose name is it? I've asked the girls several times, "Are you sure that isn't Jennings' detective?" Jennings and his friend, in *Jennings Goes to School*, start to write a detective story, and they have quite a discussion on what to name their super sleuth. They decide it has to be a two-syllable first name and a one-syllable last name; all respectable detectives have names like that. Sherlock Holmes, Sexton Blake, Nelson Lee, Dixon Hawke. So, Smudley Croak. But "*No!*" Jill shrieks as she corrects me again, raising her nose out of *Lord of the Rings*, volume three, "Jennings' detective was *Flixton Slick!*" So maybe Smudley Croak is my own attempt at a detective, or at a name as good for a frog as Warty Bliggins is for a toad, or Jerry McCormic for an ant. I hope it's my invention. I rather like it.

Often your characters' names will shape your story. When a book begins, "Once there were four little rabbits and their names were Flopsy, Mopsy, Cottontail, and Peter," you know immediately that the story's going to be about Peter, and he will be Different. I used this when Betsy in *Ghost Boat* told a story about sunfish: "Their names were Sunny, Honey, Funny, Bunny, Runny, Stripey . . . and Phil." Sure enough, the hero of the tale is Phil. But sometimes your story will shape your characters. You may have to change their names after a bit, to make them fit the type of people (or creatures) they're growing into.

A good place to flex your naming muscles is to work on the Old Woman in the Shoe. My sisters and I used to draw innumerable shoes, working out the architecture and how everyone managed to live there, and populating the pictures with many active children, all of whom had to be named. I recall one of my girls was Rosemary, my favorite name at the time. A while ago I tried a Shoe ABC, using names from A to Z, some common, some unusual, and telling what each brat did that finally caused the old woman to lose her self control. "Tom was a tattle and Tim was a tease; Ulysses drew pictures on both of his knees; Veronica wouldn't let anyone in" (picture: long line before the bathroom door); "Wilkins and Watkins created a din" (picture: tug of war with the cat, all three yowling). Nobody's wanted to publish it yet, but it was fun to do.

And a good place to listen to the music of names is on Angel Record 3582-B (35650-651), *Music for Children*, by Carl Orff and Gunild Keetman, the first side. The children making the record chant a sequence of persons' names, and then of trees and flowers. It's a delight to hear, and will make you want to try your own melodious listings.

Titles are names of another sort. For me, either a title is very easy and obvious — like *Missing Melinda* and *The Ghost Boat* — or I have a terrible time thinking up a good one. *Julie's Secret Sloth, The Paleface Redskins, The Taste of Spruce Gum* were all struggles. With *Spruce Gum* we wound up sending telegrams back and forth, my editor and I, and somebody at Little, Brown finally thought up the title just as the book was going to press. Its working title for six years had been *Tough as Tripe,* which expressed one part of the story, but not the whole thing. Now it seems as though *Spruce Gum* never had any other title, it's so just-right.

You have power over names. But names also have power over you. If you've ever screamed back at tormentors, "Sticks and stones can break my bones but names can never hurt me!" you know the power of names to hurt. A friend of ours had a perfectly good name, Oscar, but discovered when he was in the Army that this was a "joke" name. A sergeant would look down the list of soldiers and fasten on him and other men with "joke" names for all the dirty jobs. So he switched to his middle name, Bill, and slipped into comfortable anonymity. He had the power to change his name, but sometimes a person doesn't. A curly-headed little girl was a newcomer to one of our children's third grades. On the first day the name "Dracula" got attached to her, and stuck. I don't know if her classmates meant to be cruel, but by the time the teacher and other parents realized what was going on, it was too late. They tried; sympathetic classmates were alerted to help, but things couldn't be made right again. After six months the family picked up and moved to another school district, all on account of a name.

Names can also heal. Pet names, loving names, special nicknames, friendly names. Just your own name said in a certain tone or with a certain pronunciation. For some reason or other our girls, when they're feeling harmonious toward Jill, call her by her name spelled backwards: Llij. The same for Elspeth: Thepsle. I especially like it when a particular friend calls me Jacqueline with the French pronunciation.

Naming something can make you feel different toward it, change your attitude. We had a rat living in our house, a slippery daredevil who eluded every trap. We didn't want to put out poison because Elspeth was a baby, and also there were squirrels and chippies around. He made us shudder every time we saw him or the filthy evidence of his presence. Until somebody referred to him as Templeton. Immediately, he became "our" rat, and we watched him with almost benevolent interest — and actually mourned when his foot finally slipped and he succumbed to a trap.

Or take the story of the awesome sisters in the myth of Perseus, as told by Charles Kingsley in *The Heroes*:

> . . . till he came to the edge of the everlasting night, where the air was full of feathers, and the soil was hard with ice; and there at last he found the three Gray Sisters, by the shore of the freezing sea, nodding upon a white log of driftwood, beneath the cold white winter moon; and they chaunted a low song together, "Why the old times were better than the new."
>
> There was no living thing around them, not a fly, not a moss upon the rocks. Neither seal or sea-gull dare come near, lest the ice should clutch them in its claws. The surge broke up in foam, but it fell again in flakes of snow, and it frosted the hair of the three Gray Sisters, and the bones in the ice-cliff above their heads. They passed the eye from one to the other, but for all that they could not see; and they passed the tooth from one to the other, but for all that

they could not eat; and they sat in the full glare of the moon, but they were none the warmer for her beams. And Perseus pitied the three Gray Sisters; but they did not pity themselves.

Contrast this with Hawthorne's version of the same story in *A Wonder Book*. He takes the three gray sisters and names them: Nightmare, Shakejoint, and Scarecrow. Immediately they become lessened, objects of ridicule. Their awesomeness disappears, the story becomes comic. I wonder, if Kingsley had named the sisters in the above passage, perhaps Hoarfrost, Shadow, and Greylock: wouldn't they be less mystic, more familiar, simply by being named?

In the Hebrew scriptures, the name of God was too sacred to be written in any symbols. The writers made letters that stood for the name that stood for God, and now we read Jehovah or Yahweh in our translations, but nobody knows what it really is.

In 1911 an Indian stumbled into a compound in California, the last Indian untouched by white culture in North America. He had stayed hidden for many years. Two books tell about him, both by Theodora Kroeber, whose husband befriended and sheltered him: *Ishi, Last of His Tribe*, a children's novel, and *Ishi in Two Worlds*, a scholarly account. You'll find these are important books for you for many more reasons than the discussion of Yani tribal naming customs. But that part is very interesting: "Ishi" was not Ishi's true name. It was given to him by Professor Kroeber. Because the newspapers and public insisted on a name, he had to be called something. People could not understand that Ishi's culture did not permit him to speak his own name, and there was no one else left to pronounce it.

Remember Alice's confusion in Wonderland, when she doesn't know her name?

"I'm sure I'm not Ada," she said, "for her hair goes in
such long ringlets, . . . and I'm sure I can't be Mabel, for
I know all sorts of things, and she, oh, she knows such a
very little! . . . If I'm Mabel, I'll stay down here! It'll be no
use their putting their heads down and saying, 'Come up
again, dear!' I shall only look up and say, 'Who am I, then?
Tell me that first, and then, if I like being that person,
I'll come up: if not, I'll stay down here till I'm somebody
else. . . .' "

What Alice is saying here about herself and names is
going into the heart of names' greatest power. In some
mystical, magical way our names, these symbols for ourselves, *are* us.

The power of names impressed me when I was writing
a paper on cylinder seals recently. Sumerians and other
peoples in the Near East, as early as three thousand years
before Christ, wore small cylinders of stone around their
necks or wrists, on which their names or signs were en-
graved. When they had to sign a legal document or letter,
they'd roll their cylinder across the wet clay tablet, and
it would identify them. Over the years these little seals
came to have the properties of amulets, talismans, magical
protective pieces. They represented the person, like a written name. In many ways they *were* the person.

In *Old Possum's Book of Practical Cats*, T. S. Eliot talks
about naming cats:

> *The Naming of Cats is a difficult matter,*
> *It isn't just one of your holiday games;*
> *You may think at first I'm as mad as a hatter*
> *When I tell you, a cat must have THREE*
> *DIFFERENT NAMES.*

He goes on to say that a cat needs a sensible, everyday
name, such as Victor or Jonathan, George or Bill Bailey;

TURN NOT PALE, BELOVED SNAIL

and also a name that's particular, peculiar, and more digni-
fied, which never belongs to more than one cat, such as
Bombalurina or Jellylorum.

> But above and beyond there's still one name left over,
> And that is the name that you never will guess;
> The name that no human research can discover —
> But the cat himself knows, and will never confess.
> When you notice a cat in profound meditation,
> The reason, I tell you, is always the same:
> His mind is engaged in a rapt contemplation
> Of the thought, of the thought, of the thought of
> his name:
> His ineffable effable
> Effanineffable
> Deep and inscrutable singular Name.

What is that ineffable third name? For us it may be our
given name, George or Bill, Alice or Mabel, or our nick-
name, or our full name — look at the way HARRIET M.
WELSCH carefully prints out her name on every paper,
and also H*Y*M*A*N K*A*P*L*A*N in three colors with
stars, in *The Education of H*Y*M*A*N K*A*P*L*A*N*
— or it may actually be a name so sacred or hidden or
private that it is seldom if ever pronounced, like Ishi's. It
may be known only to ourselves in our heart of hearts.

The mysteriousness, the puzzle of names, is one of the
oldest controversies of philosophy. Plato, the ancient
Greek thinker, began it. Which is more real, the thing or
the name of the thing? Take his example, a chair. Is an
actual chair more real than its name, "chair," the idea of
a chair? An actual chair is touchable, sittable, when it
hasn't lost a leg, when it hasn't a ribbon across the arms
in a museum. But the name "chair," the idea, or "ideal" as
Plato calls it, is always sittable. It is perfect chairness. The
cane bottom will never wear out. Goldilocks will never

166

smash it to smithereens. It is realler, more "chair," than the variety of chairlike objects it is naming.

This might be easier to understand in something you can't touch. Take "democracy." Is the name democracy "realler" than actual democracy? We know what we mean by the word, everybody participating equally. But in practice, everybody doesn't, or can't, or isn't allowed to. There are many flaws in democracy of this sort, but there are no flaws in the ideal of democracy. Plato believed that the ultimate reality is the name, the ideal. The things themselves are the shadows.

William James, a much more recent thinker, talks of the importance of names. To a baby, he says, the world is a big buzzing confusion. Gradually he begins to sort it out. He puts names to things, and the world starts coming to order. Think back to Adam — why did God set him to work immediately, naming things? Weren't there much more important things to be done, with the world so new and all?

This chapter can only begin to go into the fascination and implications of naming. The philosophy, history, meanings, what you can learn about other matters from studying names: all these have filled many books. You can read about how people once didn't have last names, and in some cultures still don't. How surnames developed, such as by parentage (Jackson), occupation (Cook, Wheelwright), place (Hill, Dell), physical features (Short). You'll learn to recognize periods of history by names: a little cemetery near our Vermont cottage has tombstones for Epaphras, Elihu, Philena, Hilah, Jared, Aurora, Josiah, Obediah, Zariah. You can look in the phone book and have living proof that America really has been a melting pot of different cultures and countries: Olaf Duvall, Kevin Karinski.

But this much may be enough to interest you in names and naming, in thinking how we affect them and they affect us. What if we didn't have a name? We'd be pretty unsure, like Alice, or the nameless migrant boy in Ester Wier's *The Loner*. He began to get a sense of self only when he was given a name. It also happened that way to the "creep" in Tove Jansson's *Tales from Moomin Valley*, who was so small that he didn't have a name. Snufkin rather grudgingly gives him one:

> "Listen. Er. That name you asked for. What about Teety-woo, for instance. Teety-woo, don't you see, a light beginning, sort of, and a little sadness to round it off."
>
> The little creep stared at him with yellow eyes in the firelight. It thought its name over, tasted it, listened to it, crawled inside it, and finally turned its snout to the sky and softly howled its new name, so sadly and ecstatically that Snufkin felt a shiver along his back.
>
> Then a brown tail disappeared in the brambles, and all was silent.

When Snufkin returns later, to apologize for being gruff, Teety-woo is putting up a bark nameplate over his door, and is really too busy to listen:

> "I've moved away from home and begun living! It's so exciting! You see, before I had a name I just used to hop around, and perhaps feel this or that about this or that, and everything was simply happening around me, sometimes nice things and sometimes not nice, but nothing was real, don't you see?"
>
> Snufkin started to reply, but the creep continued:
>
> "Now I'm a person, and everything that happens *means* something. Because it doesn't only happen, it happens to *me*, Teety-woo. And Teety-woo may think this or think that about it, as the case may be — if you see what I mean?"

So . . . do you see what I mean? We each have that special feeling about our own name. Whether it's a name we like or not, it's ours. It's a fixed point, an anchor, a nameplate, in starting to find out who we are.

16

Gerk

"Hey, wait! My name is Jimmy Myers. What's yours?"

"Ophelia Gibbs," said Ophelia.

"Cordelia Gibbs," said Cordelia.

"O-feel-ya! Cor-deel-ya! What sort of comic book did your folks find *those* in?"

"Twin," Cordelia said with dignity, "I find this dull and muddy-mettled rascal most tedious."

"Be gone, you scullion" said Ophelia. "You rampallian! You fustilarian! I'll tickle your catastrophe."

Jimmy's mouth fell open.

"I cannot abide a gaping pig," Cordelia said.

They started off again.

"Hey, wait! Wait!" Jimmy ran alongside them. A grin spread over his face. "Hey, that's neat! Say some more."

"Why should we, you scullion? You rampallian? You fustilarian?" Ophelia repeated.

"Scullion!" Jimmy's tone was admiring. "Fus-cha—fuscha—"

"Fustilarian."

"Fustilarian. Hey, that's neat! Wait till I try that on the guys at school. Hey, maybe girls aren't so bad after all. Where'd you get that neat stuff?"

— From *Missing Melinda*

Where'd they get it? From their father, who got it from Shakespeare. I decided, as I was writing *Missing Melinda*, to make the father the sort of person who recited Shakespeare around the house for the love of it. So the twins' ears were soaking up Shakespearean English from birth, and their use of the words was natural to them.

We receive words into our consciousness first through our ears. Live speech, and also canned speech from radio, records, movies, TV. As we learn to read, words enter through our eyes by means of everything from books to billboards. Lately Megan's been learning Braille, which reminds me that our fingertips can introduce us to words, too. And in *The Phantom Tollbooth* they even enter by mouth: Milo has to eat his words and he wishes, as he munches the unappetizing fare of his own speech, that he'd chosen tastier ones.

(Tasting words isn't as far-fetched as it sounds, on first crunch. Jill discovered a poem last summer which started, "In the squdgy river, / Down the oozely bank . . ." I overheard her, a couple of days later, murmuring "squdgy" into her dishwater. I bet she was tasting that word!)

Words, new words, don't just come to us from outside. We all participate in creating language. A couple of years ago when Megan and Jill were at each other's throats all the time I heard Jill shriek, "I hate you! You're so yitchy and bliggy!" Instead of wading in to referee that collie-shangie I grabbed up a pencil. And at another, more tranquil time, I heard Megan's shout from up the hill, "On your merk — get serk — *gerk!*"

Words can be neat stuff, all right. They can be colorful, vigorous, exciting. But more often than not they're deadly dull. I've mentioned earlier that I love collecting bad examples of rewritten books. Some of my prizes are the *Peter Rabbit* variations. Poor Peter! What they've done to him over the years, in the name of consideration for children. Actually it's in the name of dollars; Peter Rabbit sells. Most buyers don't have the original *Peter* there in the grocery store with them, to compare with the gaudy version on the rack; they don't even know there is an original, written by Beatrix Potter back in 1902 and printed at her own expense since no publisher would take it. Anyway, the rack version is a buck or more cheaper, and it's the same story, isn't it?

No. Not most of the time. It's been "revised" or "adapted." And the excuse for doing anything to *Peter* is that "it needs simplifying." It's "too hard for small children." In my college children's literature classes I sometimes take the original *Peter* and a rewritten *Peter*, project them both on a wall, and we compare them. What hits the students most — after the difference between Potter's delicate, whimsical, accurate, and artistic drawings and the usual Disney-type rabbit cartoons — are the changes in words. Where Potter uses an interesting word, the rewrite uses a dull one; where Potter has chosen an exact word, now there is a muddy one.

The most striking example: Peter, you recall, ran to get away from Mr. McGregor, but unfortunately got his little jacket with brass buttons tangled in a gooseberry net. As he struggled, some friendly sparrows flew to him in great excitement and "implored him to exert himself." In the revised *Peter*, the birds "begged him to hurry away."

Someone usually agrees with the revision; the first way is too hard for children. But then somebody wonders what's so hard about "exert" and "implore?" Two-syllable words, both of them, and while not in the usual four-year-old vocabulary — though I heard, around the time of the musical of *Mary Poppins*, three-year-olds rattling off "supercalifragilisticexpialidocious" — their meaning is perfectly clear from the context and picture. I've yet to see a child have any trouble with that sentence, and I've read *Peter* to small and rapt listeners so often I have it memorized. Annis Duff, mother, children's book editor, and writer, tells a story in her book *Bequest of Wings*. Her young son was urging on a boat in a seashore puddle, and cried, "I implore you to exert yourself!" He'd gotten the point *and* the words.

She also comments, about a vocabulary-controlled book, one that is restricted to words on your own "level," that it was "as sober and uninteresting as rice pudding without any raisins." And that to little children, "new words are as interesting as new toys," and "*all words belong to children*," for "if their books do not have unfamiliar words tucked in like bright little surprises among the everyday ones, how in the world are they ever to accumulate a store of language to draw on . . . ?"

Like Ophelia, Cordelia, and the small Duff boy, you will learn the words you hear, and if you hear a wide variety of interesting and unusual words, especially when you're little, that's the sort of exciting and expressive vocabulary you'll develop. If you hear the same ordinary words over and over, that's how you'll end up speaking and writing.

Look for a minute at what those phrases from the two different *Peter Rabbits* are saying. Suppose you were the one caught by your buttons in a gooseberry net (as indeed you are; you become Peter when you read or hear that story: you "identify" with him) and some sparrows fly to you and beg you to hurry away? You'd retort, "You nincompoops, can't you see I'm trying to?" While if they urged you on in your efforts, implored you to exert yourself, their concern might help you make that final twist to rid yourself of your little blue jacket (quite new). Beatrix Potter's words are precise. They're also delightful: all our girls, from ages two or three on, have occasionally commented, "Toothsome meal, Ma!" and then I've been pleased with both the repast and — was it Mrs. Tittlemouse?

I had an early love of words, due largely to my luck in parents. My father's use of words has always been robust, humorous, and on the earthy side. He continually tells stories, he's what's called a "raconteur," and I've taken many ideas from him. It was his sympathy for the poor overworked chickens, back when farmers began keeping hen-house lights on all night during World War II, that led eventually to my *Chicken Ten Thousand* and her melancholy life in an egg factory.

Few people speak in figures of speech, in similes, but my father is one who does. Some of his favorite phrases aren't original with him, but most, I think, are spur-of-the-moment creations. "I'm as dry as a fish flopped upon the bank." "I'm full as a tick and twice as good looking." "I'm as flat as a flea between lovers." When he found me using the family toothpaste after I'd moved away from home he exclaimed, "You kids are like Sherman marching through Georgia — you live off the land!" and as he rapped my brother's knuckles with the butt of the carving knife when Craig reached over and tried to remove a bit of marrow from the ham bone, "Enough of that! You look like you're digging out an ear!"

My mother's use of words is varied and sensitive. She writes poetry, and has set some to her own music. One of my blisses as a child was to lie under the piano while she played and sang, "If you were the moon and I were the sea . . ." She preserved for us our own use of words, in woody poem fashion. My cousin Mig said to her:

> It ain't "ain't,"
> It's "isn't,"
> Ain't it, Aunty Vera?

And in a chilly situation we all still recite my brother's prekindergarten comment:

> I'm as cold as a mouse
> Without any fur
> In the winter!

Mother recognized my word-interest and saw that it was nurtured. I asked for a dictionary and a briefcase in third grade, and got an excellent specimen of each for Christmas. The bulging leather briefcase still holds my writings from that year through college. She read out loud to us — I can yet recall the thrill and chill of *The Wizard of Oz* — and provided us with classics such as *The Water Babies* and *At the Back of the North Wind* as well as beloved unknown books I've never been able to find in any library.

One of these is still one of my all-time favorites, and deals directly with words. Some company should republish it: *The Chatterlings*, by Michael Lipman. The King of the Chatterlings believes in exact speech, and when Prince Tip o' Tongue begins to use words sloppily, the King is ready to banish him to the Red Chatterlings, who say such things as "bowl" or "saucer" when they mean "cup." Then he relents and says the Prince can be king if he can find two words that mean precisely the same thing. So the story is of Prince Tip o' Tongue's search around Chatterland for these two words, as the deadline draws ever nearer. Each pair of "synonyms" he discovers — for instance, "obtain" and "receive" — prove to be just a shade different in meaning. Finally the Prince pants in, just under the wire, with two acceptable words; the King takes off his crown, and there is rejoicing in Chatterland. I won't tell you what the words are, in case you're ever lucky enough to read the book. Yes, I will, too, but later. Keep alert for them!

In the pictures, the Chatterlings illustrate not the plot, but the difference in words. For "stop," a Chatterling is resting under a bush with his hedge clippers beside him, apparently soon to resume his task; for "quit," you see the bush, while Chatterling and clippers are disappearing in the distance. Sometimes a whole lot of words are differentiated; on one page the faces of weeping, crying, sobbing, and raging Chatterlings used to wring my heart; on another, a succession of Chatterlings stand with their backsides to us, spreading their coattails so that we can see the sad state of their usually tidy pantaloons: ragged, slit, rent, ripped, torn, frayed, and tattered.

Those pantaloons! The whole Chatterling costume I
adored when I was seven; I ached to dress like a Chatterling, but knew that even if I could reproduce the tall
feathered hat and the trim-cut coat with coattails, the
pantaloons were impossible. Now, in this stretch-tights
era, they'd be the easiest part of the costume to secure.

Mother gave me Barrie's *Sentimental Tommy* when I
was older, because she loved the Scottish dialect, and
because of a particular chapter where Tommy shows how
he feels about words. He is a poor boy who aspires to be
a writer, and competes with another boy for a university
scholarship. The teachers and examining board outside the
village classroom where the essay competition is being held
hear two pens scratching briskly at the start and then,
after a while, only one. Who has quit writing? And why?
When the time is up Tommy is still in a reverie, searching
his mind for the exact word to describe how full the
church — the kirk — was. The exam has been forgotten.
He loses the scholarship ("The time went by in a wink-
ing!") but for the moment he doesn't care: the pursuit of
the word is still uppermost. It wasn't "puckle" or "manzy"
or "flow" or "curran" — what *was* it? And at least one
examiner marks down in his mind that anyone who has
that much respect for words is the superior candidate.

From *Tommy* I, too, learned to love the colorful Scotch
dialect, and I went on to read all Barrie's *Thrums* books.
I stole *A Window in Thrums* from a dusty library at a
YMCA camp once, and like a pack rat replaced it with
five Hardy Boys mysteries. I'm sure the Hardy Boys have
been read a thousand times to Barrie's probable once, but
I sometimes wonder if I deprived some other camper who
might have read it of a life-changing experience. This is
my confession of guilt, and my atonement, if this chapter
in any way sparks your interest in either Thrums or words.

Another book whose words fascinated me — as well as

the whole powerful story — was Frances Hodgson Burnett's *The Secret Garden*, where several of the characters
speak Yorkshire dialect. For days after each rereading the
pastures surrounding our farm were transformed into
Yorkshire moors, and I went around trying to talk like
Martha and Dickon.

A few years ago I was delighted to discover the Hamilton Wright Mabie version of "Tom Tit Tot," the British
Rumpelstiltskin, told as he had heard it in the Yorkshire
dialect, and if you haven't read the *Jack Tales*, collected by
Richard Chase, you are in for a treat. These are Appa-
lachian Mountain retellings of old favorite European fairy
tales. You'll recognize "Jack and the Bean Tree" immediately; it may take you a while to find your old friend
Cinderella. The vigorous mountain expressions give these
familiar stories a whole new feeling.

One more dialect book, which is invariably watered down
in the retellings, is *Uncle Remus*, by Joel Chandler Harris.
Demi, in third grade, came rushing home one noon with
her reader, and read out loud to us a version of "Tar Baby."
She'd never heard the story before and was so thrilled with
it that she had to share it. We all enjoyed it — it's hard
completely to ruin a good story — but we got talking about
the "real" Uncle Remus, and dug out a musty copy. I
stumbled badly through one reading, but managed the dialect pretty well by the second time through, for once you
hear a word like "bimeby" spoken, what was so puzzling
on the page instantly becomes "by and by." The difference
in all the words was remarkable:

. . . the fox picked up the rabbit by the leg. He swung him around his head and threw him as hard as he could into the middle of the briar bushes.	. . . he kotch 'im by de be-hime legs en slung 'im right in de middle er de briar-patch.

. . . The next thing Brer Fox knew, his rabbit stew was sitting at the top of the hill as saucily as ever. He had been fooled again!

. . . Bimeby he year somebody call 'im, en way up de hill he see Brer Rabbit settin' cross-legged on a chinkapin log combin' de pitch outen his ha'r wid a chip. Den Brer Fox know dat he bin swop off mighty bad.

Certain authors take a huge joy in playing with language. If you, the reader, are in on the games and can understand the jokes, you'll enjoy a whole extra dimension of pleasure. Probably the greatest is Lewis Carroll, in the Alice books. The Mock Turtle doesn't study Latin and Greek in school, he learns Laughing and Grief. He also studies Reeling and Writhing, Ambition, Distraction, Uglification, and Derision; Mystery and Seography; Drawling, Stretching, and Fainting in Coils — the last three taught by a conger eel. And the lessons are ten hours the first day, nine the next, and so on; that's why they're called lessons.

Alice, in *Through the Looking Glass*, gets into a long discussion with Humpty-Dumpty on words. Says Humpty,

". . . They've a temper, some of them — particularly verbs: they're the proudest — adjectives you can do anything with, but not verbs — however, *I* can manage the whole lot of them! Impenetrability! That's what *I* say!"

"Would you tell me, please," said Alice, "what that means?"

"Now you talk like a reasonable child," said Humpty Dumpty, looking very much pleased. "I meant by 'impenetrability' that we've had enough of that subject, and it would be just as well if you'd mention what you mean to do next, as I suppose you don't mean to stop here all the rest of your life."

"That's a great deal to make one word mean," Alice said in a thoughtful tone.

"When I make a word do a lot of work like that," said Humpty Dumpty, "I always pay it extra."

Looking Glass also contains the famous poem "Jabberwocky." It's perfectly understandable, even though the words are a mystery:

> *'Twas brillig, and the slithy toves*
> *Did gyre and gimble in the wabe:*
> *All mimsy were the borogoves,*
> *And the mome raths outgrabe....*

Norton Juster's *The Phantom Tollbooth* is also filled with wordplay. Milo's whole journey is an exposé of the absurdity and delight of much of our speech, as well as our reason. His visit to the Kingdom of Dictionapolis, where the whole marketplace sells words ("Get your fresh-picked ifs, ands and buts!"), his meeting with Faintly Macabre, the not-so-wicked Which, the Spelling Bee, the Everpresent Wordsnatcher, the Terrible Trivium, and all the other fantastic characters, elevate him, for me, to a spot in the pecking order somewhat under Alice and considerably above Dorothy.

The author James Thurber had great fun with words. In *The Wonderful O* every item in the Kingdom with an *o* in its name is banished, so that cake is allowed but not cookies; and everyone must speak without using a single *o*. In *The Thirteen Clocks* a tale-teller warns, "He will slit you from your guggle to your zatch." We don't know what parts of the anatomy those are, but we certainly get the idea that there's a pretty long and devasting slit we're going to get if we don't beware. And the King of Yarro says, "Weep for me, maiden, for I am ludicrous and laughable, with my foot caught in this trap. I am no longer ert, for I have lost my ertia." What's ertia? The opposite of inertia, of course.

And a final author: Recently I was visiting friends, and one of them brought me a book for us to enjoy together, one of a popular series about a human-type bear who lives with a rather colorless human family and is constantly getting into scrapes. The chapter we read went on and on — big words, even interesting words aplenty, but strung together so tediously, and all saying so little, that I began condensing paragraphs, and then skipping bigger and bigger chunks. Finally I said, "Josie, I'm bored silly, let's read this instead," and grabbed up a *Just So Stories*. What a relief to be back with the great gray-green greasy Limpopo River, all set about with fever trees, and the camel who lived in the middle of the Howling Desert, when the world was so new-and-all, and:

> Hear and attend and listen; for this befell and behappened and became and was, O my Best Beloved, when the Tame animals were wild. The Dog was wild, and the Horse was wild, and the Cow was wild, and the Sheep was wild, and the Pig was wild — as wild as wild could be — and they walked in the Wet Wild Woods by their wild lones. But the wildest of all the wild animals was the Cat. He walked by himself, and all places were alike to him.

That's from "The Cat that Walked by Himself." Notice what simple words Kipling uses on the whole, mostly one-syllable, well-known ones. But look how he puts them together!

Just as a baker needs eggs and flour, sugar and milk, to make a cake, and a carpenter needs wood, bricks, and nails to build a house, so a writer can't make a poem or a story without words. But the best raw materials in the world have to be put together well or you'll have a soggy cake or a rickety house. The words you use and the way you put them together result in your *style*. Some writers, as you know, are pretty soggy or rickety. Others are Krumgold and Kingsley and Kipling.

The trouble with the watered-down classics is that the adaptors change both the words and how they're put together, as in *Uncle Remus,* to make them "easy" for all the children whose brains and hearts and taste they pretend to respect. This ruins the unique style of the book, which is every bit as important as the story. The books all come out alike, homogenized. I've seen *Oliver Twist* "adapted" to Dick-and-Jane English, but once in a while the rewriter was forced to use a special Dickensian word or phrase for which there was no substitute. The bit is ridiculously out of place, but by far the most interesting spot on the page! A poppy patch blooming in the middle of a barren supermarket lot.

The writer's materials, unlike the baker's or carpenter's, are free. Interesting words don't cost any more than dull ones. Nobody's going to say, except in *Tollbooth* and *Alice,* "Here's a box of highly polished adverbs, Grade A jumbo, 63¢ a dozen." It's a sorry thing that with the choice of so many hundreds of thousands of words, so much writing is dreary.

On second thought, though, let me take back some of the free part. Certain words perhaps aren't free. A student told me his sixth-grade teacher tore up his stories because they were "weirdo" — about subjects that made the teacher uncomfortable: suicide and death. A friend of Megan's used vulgarities and swear words in an essay, and got booted out of English class. I paid the price when a book club in Ohio didn't choose *Spruce Gum* for their recommended list, because the loggers said "damn." I defend anyone's right, even children's, to use taboo words and subjects in the right place at the right time. You can even use them at other times, but that's bad art, and for that I'll fault you. I won't tear up your stories, though.

I've found that most vulgar words and swear words are pretty boring after the initial shock has worn off. It takes imagination to think up vivid and interesting oaths and insults. The master here is Hergé, the French writer of hardcover, magnificent comic books, the *Tintin* series. When things go a little wrong for Captain Haddock, a lovable sot, he cries, "Blistering barnacles!" A bit worse and it becomes "Billions of blistering barnacles!" and so it builds up until finally, when things are as bad as they can possibly be, he roars, "Billions of bilious blue blistering barnacles in a thundering typhoon!" When his whiskey bottle is broken by Arabs he takes out after the raiders barehanded, bawling, "Swine! Jellyfish! Tramps! Troglodytes! Toffeenoses! Savages! Aztecs! Toads! Carpetsellers! Iconoclasts! Rats! Ectoplasms! Freshwater swabs! Cannibals! Bashi-bazouks! Caterpillars! Cowards! Baboons! Parasites! Pockmarks!" I looked up troglodyte and bashi-bazouk once, figuring they were made-up words — but no, they're perfectly legitimate, with excellent meanings, and great to yell at your friends. So then I searched out a French copy of *Tintin* figuring that someone had to translate those expletives into English, and what sort of words did Hergé have in the original? I found *troglodyte* and *bashi-bazouk!*

My kids remind me here that dear little Nigel Molesworth, in *How to Be Topp*, is also pretty good at insulting language ("you wets, you weeds"), and is well worth your attention, nor does Asterix do badly, by Toutatis!

For all my love of words, there was a period when I hated them. Fourth grade was a horrible year. That's when we learned not only long division but how to use the dictionary. I'd taught myself earlier, but too many schools both then and now don't take into account what a particular person already knows. In my fourth grade we all did the same exercises whether we needed them or not.

For dictionary drill — the very name makes me wince —

we had a list of words and we'd look them up as fast as we could and copy the definitions. No relationship to our other studies or to our living, no browsing time for one tuft of interesting words to lead us to another more succulent one. Just flip, flip, flip, and copy.

Times haven't changed too much. A number of "Miseries" that I've encountered recently from schoolchildren have been dictionary ones: "Misery is when you're naughty, chewing gum or something, you have to write thirty words and definitions." "When we're bad we have to copy a page from the dictionary." "Misery is when we make noise we have to look up 'quiet' and write its pronunciation and definition fifty times." Now there's a way to make word-lovers of all of you!

Dictionary games are a better way. There are a number; in the one I like best one person, "it," chooses an unfamiliar word from the dictionary and announces it to the group. Everyone then makes up a definition and writes it down in best dictionary fashion, while "it" writes down the real definition. He collects the slips, reads them all aloud, and there is then a vote on each definition — who thinks which is the authentic one? "It," of course, doesn't vote, only smiles enigmatically. I guess the winner is the one who chooses correctly most often, but the fun is in the ingenuity of the definitions more than in winning. One night someone selected "scut," and here are the meanings that emerged:

1. a viscous jelly.
2. scut, n. discharge from infections of the inner ear
3. scut, n. A stubby erect tail, such as that of a hare, rabbit, or deer.
4. scut, n. a knot in a fishnet, from *scutting,* making fishnets.
5. scut, n. an insult so subtle that it is not perceived as such by the receiver.

6. scut, n. surplus, overabundance
7. scut (n) — section of ship's hold used for stowaways discovered on early English vessels
8. scut, n. unimportant materials, disposable goods. Archaic: useless rewards.

Which is the right one? Interesting that no one chose to make it a verb. Can you make up what it means "to scut"? (Past tense of "scoot"?)

A stubby tail is correct. Mine was #5, I'm rather proud of it. I've since heard the phrase "scut-work" used for unpleasant, undesirable chores (usually assigned). Jill read this page and said, "That's the game we were playing when I learned 'glumaceous'!"

Before leaving dictionaries, our kids discovered a remarkable one several years ago. Demi was complaining about children's dictionaries. "Why do they always put in the *ordinary* words? I want to make a dictionary with the *extraordinary* words!" Her father told her it'd already been done, though it contains the ordinary, too, and that it was the Oxford English Dictionary, called affectionately the OED by scholars the world over. We, indeed, possessed an old set of the Shorter OED, which he'd found at a second-hand book store. The girls began poring through it and came up with such tidbits as:

collieshangie — noisy quarrel, confused fight
natterjack — a British species of toad, having a light yellow stripe down the back
olam — a vast period of time, an age

The OED also goes into the origin of words, which is an absorbing study, and gives examples of when and how a certain word has been used in the past. It was in the OED that I solved the mystery of "fills." When I was writing *Spruce Gum*, I listened to Grandma Vi tell about the lumber camp, and took down her words as fast as I could manage. She described the accident where the train hit the buggy and Mr. Reed and Mrs. Vincent were killed, but her husband Bert, Uncle Charles in the story, was saved: "Bert was just plain lucky. He was settin' on that little canvas seat, sort of ahead of the other two, and had aholt of the reins, and when Old Tom saw that train bearing down about to hit he gave a leap and broke his fills and jerked Bert right along with 'im."

I didn't ask her what fills were; from the context I assumed they were part of the harness. I put the description in my book just as she told it. The final copy came back from the copy editor with a big circle around the word, with the inquiry, "Fills? The insides of sausages?" I looked up my notes and confirmed that "fills" was the exact word I'd heard from Grandma Vi. So I knew it was okay, but by then I was curious and intrigued. What *were* "fills"? I could have called Vi and asked her, but that was long distance to Vermont, so first I looked the word up in the usual dictionaries, *Webster's, American College,* and so on. Sure enough, in all of them "fills" were only the fillings of sausages. After four or five tries it occurred to me to look in our Shorter OED and there it was: "sausage fillings" first, but then, "fill: now dialect. variation of thill: the space between the shafts." It was but a flip over to "thill," and there I found out: "thill: the pole or shaft by which a wagon, cart or other vehicle is attached to the animal drawing it, especially one of the pair of shafts between which a single draught animal is placed."

I felt like the winner of a treasure hunt as I wrote the definition back to the copy editor, and filed away "thills-fills" as a little glowworm of pleasure to irradiate some dim corner of my soul when it needed it.

There are other books that go specifically into the fascination of words. There are slang dictionaries, books of origins, histories of the English language. *You English Words* by John Moore introduced us to "quockerwodger," a doll whose legs and arms fly out when you pull a string, hence also a politician who can be manipulated, and "ostrobogulous," meaning — well, a certain Mr. Neuberg once exclaimed it when he heard that someone had called him a dromedary; in his outrage he probably made it up. Till it was found in Mr. Moore's book it was recorded only in its original source. I put it in my *Ghost Boat* because we were all so intrigued by it, and now it's here. Maybe other people are using it, too. Thus do words spread and gain popularity, or wane and disappear.

So what are your own pleasures in words? How might you make your speech and writing more toothsome? Try listening to words used vividly, if you can find someone like my father; listen to someone read aloud *The Wind in the Willows* and *Tintin* and other books with splendid words and great style. Read them out loud yourself.

You might taste words like "squdgy" to see how they feel on your lips and tongue. I find the physical effort it takes to say a word is pleasurable. Try combustible. Squash. Schmaltz. Fussbudget. Asphyxiate. Rolls-Royce. Whiskey. Azure. Oyster. Lissome. Smooch. The children on the Orff record described in "Warty Bliggins" are enjoying the glidey feel of saying, "pear tree, pear tree," the puff of the lips on "apple tree, apple tree," and the vigor of using their lips and tongues on "blackthorn, buckthorn, hawthorne, poplar" — rough, catchy words. They finish, "saxifrage, goldenrod, rose . . ." and "rose," with only four letters, takes longer to say than "blackthorn" with ten.

You could make a list of the ten most beautiful words you know. A dictionary maker — was it Mr. Funk or Mr. Wagnalls? — listed "dawn, hush, lullaby, murmuring, tranquil, mist, luminous, chimes, golden, melody." Someone retorted, "Aha, you're confusing a word's beautiful *meaning* with how it sounds! What is more beautiful *sounding* than 'cellar door'?" For many a word ordinary, or even unpleasant in meaning has a delightful sound: Trichinosis. Leprosy. Hemophilia. Appendectomy. Vomit. And some words that mean pleasant things may offend your ear.

The sound and taste and feel of words make it hard for me to be a speed reader. We're all urged to read fast and get the meaning. Otherwise, we'll never catch up with the amount of print we have to cover these days. I agree it would be good to polish off most newspapers in five minutes, or even two. But some things shouldn't be read swiftly. Poetry. Or can't be, like mathematics or philosophy or the directions for putting together a wagon. Yet I don't recall any teacher of mine ever making distinctions in reading rate. It was go fast, don't move your lips, don't hear the words.

In certain reading I *want* to hear the words! I even go back over paragraphs to hear the words again. And I feel a little irritated when someone reads in an hour and a half a book I've taken five or six years to write. Maybe the words and style aren't the finest, but almost every word and how it fits with its fellows has been lovingly thought about. I don't like them slighted.

Think up your own words for special occasions, special things. A Wisconsin teacher wrote me that she'd once called those annoying curls that are left when you rip a page out of a spiral notebook "foozies," or maybe it was "foozles" — take your pick — but anyway, the word spread through the whole school like wildfire.

Recall your family made-up words. When Elspeth was just learning to write and spell she took a sister's record book and on a blank page recorded several scurrilous remarks about her sibling, finishing up with "You snote! (snicer, snicer)." The first word shouldn't be difficult to interpret; the second two are "snicker, snicker," and when we use them — as we do frequently — we pronounce them to rhyme with "slicer." "Sneep" is one my grandmother used, probably brought over from England with her a hundred years ago, and I never knew it was a family word till I used it in public and found blank looks. It means that you feel pretty small and sort of embarrassed and rueful and — well, *sneeped*. If you've had your comeuppance, you're sneeped. And now, I'm sneeped — or rather, sneaped, for as I wrote the above sentences, so soon after telling about "thills" and the OED, I thought, "Oh-oh, maybe I better go look up 'sneep,' too!" And there it is, not "sneep" but "sneap," and it *must* be the same word even though my understanding is slightly different: "sneap — now *dialect* and *archaic*. 1. to nip or pinch. 2. to check, repress; to snub, reprove, chide. A rebuke, reproof."

But I'm not so sneaped that I can't appreciate the words I've just discovered flanking my object: a *sneaksby* is a mean-spirited person, a paltry fellow; a *sneak-up* is a sneak and a shirk; to *sneb* is to snub; a *sneck* is a door-latch, and hence a *sneck-drawer* is one who draws the sneck or latch stealthily, and therefore is a crafty, flattering, or sly fellow; to *sned* is to lop off a branch, and I'll finish with *snee* (to cut): see SNICKERSNEE; and that's a word my grandma always used when we were naughty — "I'll snickersnee you!" — except I always called it "snickersneeze." Probably because it tickled my catastrophe!

So are you ready? It's an easy race, the course will take you into all sorts of fascinating places, and everybody gets a prize. On your merk . . . get serk . . . *gerk!*

17

How (Maybe) to Rewrite a Book
— or Anything

W HILE I'VE BEEN WORKING on this book this summer my
talk with friends around the lake has frequently turned to
writing, and children's writing, since that's where my mind
has been a lot of the time. Carol, Heather's mother — you
met Heather in "Eavesdrop!" — told me last night, "Remember that book Heather was working on last summer
and getting so much pleasure out of? Well, her teacher asked
all the kids to bring in any creative writing they'd been
doing at home, and Heather gave her her beloved *Alone on
an Island*. And do you know what that teacher did?"

"What?" I asked, knowing pretty well and dreading the answer.

"When Heather got it back it was all red-penciled: spelling, grammar corrected, she'd even changed words to ones she thought sounded better. Heather hasn't touched it since."

In graduate school a friend told me about an experience she'd had as a sixth-grader. She wrote what I consider to be an imaginative simile, drawn out of her own childhood images since she lived in New York City: "My father and I are as alike as two tugboats." The teacher read this to the class and called it ridiculous. "*People* aren't like tugboats!" Jimmy said she was so crushed she'd never written anything "creative" after that, either.

A Rockford teacher told this on herself. A student gave her a story he'd written and "I took his paper and made some corrections on it and when he saw it he grabbed it off my desk and said, almost crying, 'What'd you go messing around with my story for?' I haven't used red pencil on creative writing since."

Last year Megan's teacher used a book of photographs to stimulate creative writing. For one lesson the assigned picture was a distant view of two people among trees on what appeared to be a mountaintop. The kids were to write a third of a story that day, the second third the next, and the final third the day after. Agreed, it's a sappy assignment. Megan wrote a long paragraph. The teacher read it over her shoulder and said, "Mm, that's a very good beginning." "Actually," said Megan, "it's finished. It's all I have to say." The teacher argued with her and ordered her to write some more. Megan said she'd start over and write another story the way the teacher wanted it, but this particular one was done. "No, you won't," said the teacher. "You have to finish *this* one." Megan didn't say anything more, the teacher sighed and walked away, and Megan handed in a new story. I heard this with some indignation and asked to see the old story. Here it is:

> It's late afternoon and the two have wandered up to the top of the rounded mountain alone. . . . The evening sunlight shines through the mist making the whole world golden. A silver creek slides across the mossy rocks, and a trout glides under the cool trees. They are studying a velvet mushroom, orange against the deep green moss. Both feel a distance, while yet a nearness, prolonging the words which must be said.

I support Megan, that it's finished. It's just not a "story." It's more a tone poem, a mood piece, and it isn't the length the teacher wanted. But the problem was in the lesson and the expectations.

Well, I'm mixing up writes and rewrites a little, but my main purpose, I think, is to make the teachers the villains in those little dramas, which aren't little at all if you are the victim. For it's mainly the teachers who want the rewrites, and certain sorts of writes to begin with, occasionally a parent, ever anybody else? — and they also want everything all neatened up properly. And they are the ones who have their hooks into you, Beloved Snail, who can scare you out of the dance.

There are, of course, exceptions, but too many teachers don't want rewrites for getting even better, deeper writing. Their sneaky purpose is usually to perfect the form, to use this way to teach you paragraphing, etc., etc., etc. They're only secondarily interested in what you say, if they're interested at all. I'm not against good paragraphing or the spelling necessary to get your message across. I've done a couple of rewrites of this manuscript and corrected all my spelling mistakes, I think. Likewise, by my standards, my paragraphing is okay. I *am* against wrecking up people's creativity, especially kids'. Suppose you showed your new-

born baby, still red and wrinkly and slippery, to a baby
expert and he said, "Well, it's a baby — probably — but its
nose is too long and its rump is too short and the color's a
shade off, and . . ." A *real* baby expert doesn't treat you or
your babies in that manner.

But there's one other person I haven't mentioned, who
might want a rewrite, and that's you. Why might you want
a rewrite? I love the Peanuts cartoon where Charlie Brown
says to Linus, about scouting the rival ball team, "Now the
first question that probably pops into your mind is, 'Why
does this job need to be done?' " And Linus replies, "No,
the first question that pops into my mind is, 'Why me?' "
Anyway, here are some reasons I'd hope you'd have, to
make you want to do a rewrite; they're my own reasons
for rewriting:

1. Because you love what you've written, and you want
to work on it some more. The first writing has brought up
additional thoughts, has stirred the still waters of the well
of your subconscious, and now there are all sorts of leaves
and stuff swirling around that want to get in. Or you've
made, say, a rough statue, and now you pull some clay off,
discard it or put it elsewhere, add new clay, change pits to
knobs and knobs to pits, smooth the thing in some places,
leave it rough for texture in others . . . loving the feel on
your hands, enjoying the improvement as well as the continuation of your creation.

2. Because you love it so much you want to share it with
others, and therefore all the etcs. need attention — your
spelling, your crummy handwriting, etc. When Ned Stone
was five, he wrote his first story, about a dinosaur baby who
lived in a mud hole. The mother dinosaur told him it was
time to leave the mud hole. "What?" said the baby. "Leave
the *world?*" Ned's parents helped him fix up his story in
book form, and he illustrated it. As he left for kindergarten
carrying the finished work, he turned at the end of the

walk and said to them, *"This is my proud moment."* He loved what he'd created, and he was anticipating sharing it.

So how do you do a rewrite? One way is to do the whole thing over without looking at the original. I rewrote *Chicken Ten Thousand* that way, after a many-year gap. More usual, I read over what I have, think, "That bit's *good,* it says it exactly the way I want," and then leave that bit, and go on to the spots that don't sound right, which I either cut out completely, or muss around with till they do sound right.

Sound right? What, no rules? That's where all the rest of this book comes in, the smelling, tasting, seeking out a variety of experiences, looking, listening. All these things will help you to know when your writing rings true, sounds right — sits right in your guts — and when it doesn't, you'll try again, or move parts around, until it does. Or at least as long as you care. If you don't care, don't rewrite.

If you follow rules, or at least the ones I used to try to follow, you run into trouble. I told you in "Eavesdrop!" about *Spruce Gum* and the copy editor. You lose the "sounding right." Take the poem, "Love don't make a difference," in the "Woodies" chapter. No teacher should've made Kenneth change that to "proper" English and none, thank goodness, did. Proper English teaches you not to write in half sentences, either. Like this one. Well, people talk in half sentences. Think in fragments. If we follow speech, we can't slavishly follow rules.

That doesn't mean we don't bother to learn basic syntax. There are certain constructions you have to follow if you want your writing understood. "The dog bit the postman" is quite different from "The postman bit the dog." But a lot of grammar rules are really matters of style, and as Winston Churchill said when some editor circled a preposition at the end of a Churchillian sentence, "This is the sort of impertinence up with which I will not put." We should learn the rules as a means to an end, and not let them boss us. Humpty Dumpty in *Through the Looking Glass* had the right idea, except that he's talking about words:

> "The question is," said Alice, "whether you *can* make words mean so many different things."
> "The question is," said Humpty Dumpty, "which is to be master — that's all."

The best way to learn how to master rules, in my opinion, is not through sterile exercises, but through working on vital and interesting creations. Then, in the context of your own writing, you'll see why a rule is valuable and perhaps was made in the first place, or why in this instance it should be modified or ignored. I learned in music theory never to write a series of notes called parallel fifths, yet music, good music, is full of the critters. You just have to know where to use them.

I suggest that after you've worked on something awhile and it doesn't fall right, and you're beginning to be discouraged, or frustrated, or angry, rather than crumpling up your paper and flinging it from you, you put it away for a bit — an hour, a day, a week. Let your subconscious take over for you and work on the problem. Frequently it will figure it all out while you're doing something else. Even if it doesn't, when you come back to the spot you'll see it from some other angle, and often this is enough. I use this same technique, coming at it afresh, in slogging along at a rewrite: I call it snowplowing.

The plow gets to the bank and can't push it any farther. Then it goes back, revs up, comes barreling along the plowed snow, hits the bank, and goes through — or at least a little farther. I find that rereading the earlier paragraphs or pages, even starting from the beginning of a chapter, and coming up to the hard spot pretending it isn't there, creeping up on it, taking it by surprise, and then when I get to it, *not* reading it (for this puts me back in the same old rut, same frame of reference) but instead writing new stuff like mad on the strength of what's gone before — this gets me a few sentences farther, sometimes right through the bank. And this is a heck of a paragraph, don't you think? Which definitely needs rewriting.

Okay. I'm now doing the rewrite of this "Rewrite" chapter. Some friends who have read the manuscript in rough draft have suggested that since this book is somewhat concerned with writing, I not do a rewrite at all. This will show what an unrewritten, unedited book looks like, with crossouts, notes in the margin, evidences of reconsiderations. I can see some value in that, but now that I've come back to the book, after quite an interval from the original writing, what I've written and how I've written it makes me squirm in too many places. It's like seeing a woman in those big fat hair rollers. She shouldn't be out on the street. However, for whatever it's worth, I've left the paragraph about snowplowing as I first wrote it, like a fly in amber. I'll take another crack at it here:

I reread the earlier paragraphs, or even start from the beginning of the chapter, and approach the impasse pretending it isn't there. I want to take it by surprise. Then when I'm suddenly upon it, I swerve: I don't reread it, for this would keep me in the same old rut. Instead I start writing madly, on the strength of the new thrust. This often gets me a few sentences farther, sometimes right through the bank.

There, does that read any more clearly?

I've been asked, how many times do you rewrite a story? And I've heard lecturing authors say, "Next you do three or four rewrites" (gasp from the audience). Rewrites — at least mine — are like painting a picture with oils. You're probably more familiar with watercolors, but you can do certain things with oils that would wreck a watercolor: oil paints don't run, you can paint over and over a spot, or scrape the paint all off a section right down to the bare canvas. Sometimes, in an oil painting, the paint goes on a spot just right. You don't need to touch it, ever. And sometimes you just can't get it right and go over and over and over it till the paint gets so thick that you take your knife and scrape it all off in disgust and start from scratch. But you don't need to redo the whole picture, the perfect spots. Just the bad ones.

Sometimes my writing suits me the first time. It sounds real. I hardly change a word. That happened with parts of *Spruce Gum*, such as the fight between Mama and Uncle Charles, the fight between Mama and Uncle Henry. Other spots come right with a second going over, or a third. But sometimes spots have to be written over ten, fifteen times, the paint scraped off and started again. This is often true of first and last paragraphs. Probably the first and last pages of *Spruce Gum* were rewritten twenty times each. That's because beginnings and endings are so important. You're breaking into life, and then you're bowing out. At the start, your story hasn't the push in front to keep it going, or at the end, what's coming next for it to lead into. If you've ever rolled a tire, you know that starting it and stopping it are the trickiest parts; once it's going, it's going, and you just run alongside and keep it headed in the right direction.

I guess my rewriting averages out to three or four or five times, but that's like talking about the "normal" or "average" person. We're all different, every time, and there actually is no average.

When you rewrite, by the way, take a long hard look at that first paragraph, whether you need it at all. Come on your story cold. Cover the start with your hand and begin reading at the second paragraph. See if you miss anything.

Often, after struggling and struggling, I remember to do this and find my whole problem is solved by throwing the first paragraph out. It's just been the dog turning round and round before settling down.

This is also true with the last paragraph, maybe not quite so often. The story has ended, and yet we keep on writing a little bit more.

There's a joy for me in a rewrite. That first ecstacy of having a really good idea and getting it down is usually diminished, although a whole new page or chapter may rekindle it, but there is a different sort of pleasure in being a good craftsman. Of finding, the next time through, the exact word you didn't wait for the first time. Of changing a garbled idea to a clear one. Of thinking of an image for illustration where you didn't have one before, or a better one than the first one. Of sandpapering it all fine, getting out the splinters and rough edges, so that there's a deep pleasure in running your hand over it, like a cello neck. And of seeing, as my writing professor Mr. Cowden called it, "what's lying in the material."

I'd go into my session with him and we'd sit there with my scrawled pages in front of us. There'd be a faint squiggle of lead in a margin, as if someone accidentally joggled a pencil there. Mr. C. would clear his throat a little and hover his pencil over the spot, and we'd both reread it, and as I'd look at it I'd suddenly see — or slowly, it happens both ways — *what was there*. Like those pictures in *Jack and Jill* or other kids' magazines where fish and umbrellas and roller skates are hidden in tree foliage or different parts of the picture, and once you see them you marvel that you didn't see them there all the time. (This simile I just added in the rewrite; it livens things up, don't you think?) I'd see what I was saying that needed more saying, or what I wasn't saying that needed saying. What was lying right there in the material that I hadn't realized.

Meanings, implications, ideas. Now *there's* a joy for you. That joy is worth a lot to me, and keeps me sustained over the dull, plodding parts.

About those last: a lot of times I have to slog till I get rolling. Once I do roll, though, those parts usually get chucked. If they're dull to me as a writer they'll be dull to you as a reader. But they've served their purpose.

I learned a valuable lesson rewriting *Palefaces*, my first major rewrite job. I didn't want to rewrite it, I loved every word, I thought: it was about my beloved Pleasant Lake and I'd tried to convey the depth of my passion about water and stars and people and growing up, and besides it was funny, built on our family's youthful skirmishes with the Boy Scouts. Why should any of it go? But Little, Brown didn't want it because it was too long, and every other company I sent it to also thought so. One even said it should be cut by two-thirds! So when Little, Brown a year later suggested I cut out a hundred pages and then they'd take it, I took a long hard look at it, to see what I could bear to part with. I began by striking out every unnecessary word. I found a lot of them. I found I didn't need as many adjectives, one or two exact ones are better than a string of them; I found adverbs are usually unnecessary; I found that a reader can follow the he sez's and she sez's without having to be told every time who's speaking. And I discovered that when I had something important to say, I had said it six times to be sure the reader got it. It really only needed to be said once. And then I found that lots of times it didn't even need to be said at all, it was right there in the conversation and the action, and the author, me, was just whacking it with a hammer to be sure the reader noticed. I began to credit the reader (you, and now me, too; I was reading it) with some brains. I'd been insulting our intelligence. And it was more fun, as a reader, to get the clues and make the point for myself.

I didn't cut anything out of *Palefaces*. I just gave it an immense squeeze job, and wrung out one hundred pages of unnecessary words. If I did it again tomorrow, I could probably get out another twenty or thirty.

Which brings me to a danger of rewriting. You can keep rewriting forever. For one thing, you get attached to your writing, you don't want it to end. So you keep on fussing and polishing. But also there's another reason. Your story is never as good as you can make it, there are better words and figures of speech you can find, there are new ideas that keep coming to you, brought on by fresh experiences, fresh reading and thinking. You cut out huge chunks, take different approaches, make radical changes. For your writing *is* you, and you're a growing, changing person so that your previous writing is never where you are now. It doesn't represent you properly. You've changed from when you wrote the first paragraph to when you wrote the last, and the writing itself has had its effect in changing you. So, you go back and update the earlier writing.

This is a special problem with kids, and Demi, Megan, and I have already given it a whack in "Me Best Thoughts." Heather talked about it today when I asked her for her version of the red pencil fiasco I described at the start of this chapter. "Well, it wasn't *just* that, why I quit writing. I reread *Alone on an Island* and the first part of it was so different. In a year, you know, I'd changed a lot, and my vocabulary had widened, and I wrote differently. . . ."

There are more changes in you between nine and ten than there will be between forty-two and forty-three, although there can be some profound changes in a year even after you've grown up; you're never set, thank God. Or if you are, it's more like Jell-O than concrete. Something can melt you.

But your ability to express yourself, to write, is growing with gigantic leaps from five to fifteen, and long works like

Heather's *will* be more "childish" at the start than at the finish. Solutions? One is, so what? Accept *Alone on an Island* for what it is, the progress of you. Another is, rewrite some, but don't expect to "even" it up. Yet another, don't try to produce long things, be content with short. A fourth is, quit it when you outgrow it, leave it unfinished and start something new. To me a journal is really the answer. It's a continuation of you, a running commentary on how you grow and change. Your stories and books can be "shaped pieces" out of your journal. And your journal you never need to finish, to give up.

I've mentioned in the "Eye" and "Mud" chapters Louisa Liske's kindergarten games. Her husband, a psychologist, put this whole changing–letting go business into words for me, after I'd been writing and rewriting *The Taste of Spruce Gum* for several years and it was more or less finished. But I was still making changes, fretting. He said something like this: "There comes a time when you've said it all, for that subject, at that time of your life. You can go on forever but it may go downhill, you go stale. The time comes when you need to decide, that's it! That it's not perfect, but it's where you were then, and are, up till nearly now; this part is done. Cut it off, end it, go on to fresh material, which will represent the you of the now and the future."

So then you quit rewriting.

REWRITING REVISITED

That last sentence seemed so definitely a last sentence that even though it wasn't intended to be, I couldn't get past it. I'll add in here what else I meant to say. Whack at the subject a little more.

There's an aspect to keeping on rewriting, and not letting go, that I hinted around the edges of but didn't hit head on, and that's fear.

In the "Warty Bliggins" chapter I talked about a name being me. Here I've been saying, my writing is also me, an extended me. The fear is, I don't want to be rejected. I want to share myself as deeply as possible, but rather than reveal myself inadequately, not be the *real* me, I keep on writing and changing to try to get it all in. So others will understand what I'm trying to say, who I am, will accept me. And it takes courage to finish something, to let someone else see it, to let it go. Because that's me showing and you might not accept me. It's a risk.

Even if I try to reveal the whole me, it is impossible for we're each of us many people — including people we don't know, and never will, fully. A leader at a communications conference described a "Johari window," which I will here oversimplify, but it'll give you the idea. The whole window is "me," and it's that lower-right-hand pane that I'm specifically thinking of, the eight-ninths of the iceberg that nobody knows:

the me I know and you know	the me you know and I don't
the me I know and you don't	the me neither of us knows

ME

But suppose I *can* reveal adequately and honestly the whole me, and you understand me wholly. Still that me, full of faults, might not be good enough for you. I repeat, it's terribly risky. For we will certainly be rejected by some-body. Somebody, understanding us or not, will red-pencil us, or ridicule us, or ignore us, or clobber us in a review.

What makes the risk necessary, by writing or by any other form of self-revelation, is that we need to reach out whether anyone meets our hand or not; if we don't, we'll shrivel up and die inside. If we do meet that hand, even if it's only one, then the risk is gloriously worthwhile and makes up for all the rest. I made a new friend after *Spruce Gum* was finished but before it was published; while we were discussing something, he threw in, "when you wrote *Spruce Gum* for children —" I interrupted, "I didn't write *Spruce Gum* for children; I wrote it for *you*." Just as I wrote *Spruce Gum* for you, O Best Beloved reader, and this book also, whether you're young or old, if somewhere in it we meet and I say anything that has meaning for you.

This may sound as though I don't want any criticism at all of any writing, mine or yours; it's too tender to touch. Not really. I do want it, but I long for a certain sort. I would hope the criticism of me, and you, would be deep criticism, honest criticism, loving criticism, the kind that would help us to grow so we'll do better next time, instead of the kind that Jimmy got, that causes us to turn pale and leave the dance. I know that's a big order. It will help to remember, no matter what quality the criticism, that critics are people, too, with strong points and weak, understand-ings and misunderstandings just like us; the teacher with the red pencil isn't God, nor is the person who writes the book review.

While writing all this I realize I've been giving two more reasons for rewriting, or for writing at all. So, summing up:

3. We want people to know us.

4. We want to know who we are ourselves.

It helps us to write our thoughts, and also to speak them, for in speaking and writing we get those thoughts out and in order that before have been hazy and amorphous. Then we can see them, where we are, who are the multiple people we are. This enables us to think some more, grow some more. We come to grips with ourselves. We become our own best critics.

FLAT CAT
or
p.s. A Small Illustration of Rewrite-Thinking

Back on page 32 I mentioned leaving blanks, or scribbling "ww" over words that aren't quite right, but will do for the time. On rewrites those blanks and words all get taken care of, and even words that seemed okay originally also come up for reconsideration.

For instance, right now I'm reading over the typed-up first draft of the "Garlic" chapter. Just passed the point, "Food is flat and tasteless —" and felt that I'd recently said some form of "taste" several times. So, what should I substitute to make it more varied? In our family we've used the phrase "cardboardy" for tasteless stuff, so I put in, in my mind, "flat and cardboardy," but that didn't seem quite right, either. It really was "tasteless" I wanted. I also discovered, after writing this brief addendum, that I'd already used "cardboard" in that chapter to describe Freddie's hamburgers, and two cardboards in a chapter — unless it's about cardboard — are too many.

But the juxtaposition of "flat" and "cardboardy" hit a key in my mind; I recalled that several times I'd passed over a blank in the "Woodies" chapter: "talk is as dull and flat as _____." I hadn't yet come up with the simile I wanted. The usual expression is "flat as a pancake," which is so ordinarily — the word is "cliché" — that nobody even thinks of a pancake when they read it. Or if they did, they might dispute the "dull" part. Pancakes after a week of cold cereal for breakfast can be quite exciting, they might argue, and I'd be inclined to agree.

What else is flat? Squashed things; my mind jumped to "squashed June bug," but while flat, that's hardly dull, either. Gooey, crunchy, a bit repulsive — but nonetheless of some interest. Also I'd used "Becky squashed my bug!" for Alison in the "Miseries" chapter, and if two cardboards are too much for one chapter, two squashed bugs are too many for one book. Yes, I know, there are a whole lot more, outside the kindergarten door in the "Toast" chapter. Those sneaked in on the very last rewrite and refused to be exterminated. I could change Alison again, but I'd already changed her from "Becky wouldn't play with me," which was what she really said. There's no law that you have to stick to the letter of the truth in a book like this.

But, "squashed June bug" led me to think of my first squashed remembrance, when a milk truck ran over a toad before our house at the Dairy, and we all sorrowfully examined the dusty, dry, flat leather shape (for we had watered that toad in our garden) and then sprinkled it with lavender talcum powder in some childish attempt to disguise death. But "flat toad" also didn't seem right, it was again too dramatic an image for a description of dullness. The problem was, I needed a dull simile.

That's why my father's "flat flea" wouldn't do, or Bob Morrow's "flat cat," either, both of which I was reminded of by "flat toad." Bob Morrow, who illustrated *The Orchestra Mice*, told me once that as kids they used to play "Flat Cat" with cats that cars ran over. You slung them like a Frisbee with a tail. But I immediately rejected that as too appalling. I'd have to explain it, and that, plus the shock, and humor of sorts, would throw the reader completely out of what I was saying.

But now, I thought, cardboard's flat and cardboard's dull. Put cardboard in that spot, "dull and flat as cardboard," and the blank is taken care of. Not a great simile, actually a pretty dull passage, but it's right and it'll do, it'll do.

18

Other People

T HIS IS THE LAST CHAPTER.

This book has mainly been talking about your own basic
inner material. I've been hoping to make you more aware
of what lies inside you and around you, more conscious of
the things that you feel or have felt keenly about, and I've
been urging you to write these things down for a variety of
reasons, one — not the most important but not the least,
either — being that these are the stuff of meaningful writing. And throughout I've been pouring out my own gut
material. How can I expect you to reveal yours, if I won't?

Besides, my own material is interesting to me, as yours is to you. I have confidence that mine will be interesting to others, as yours also will be. I've vastly enjoyed writing this book in this way; I haven't merely done it to be an example to you, for that's not a powerful enough reason for the time and effort and forgetting to take Elspeth to a birthday party.

In a book of this sort, without a continued story to give it a beginning, middle, and end, I could keep adding chapters forever. There's always more to say. One has to stop somewhere, however, and there are a few loose threads in other chapters which, if gathered, might weave a conclusion.

Remember when I talked about my grandfather, in the "Ears" chapter? How he went deaf as a young man? And how it wasn't till after he died that I gradually began to realize all the things I'd wanted to ask him? Such as, what were things like in Beaver Dam, Wisconsin, when he was a little boy? What sort of house did he live in, what did he do all day? What were his parents, my great-grandparents, like? What was his first impression of Grandma? Tell me about buying the farm, Grandpa, after you decided to leave the ministry because of your deafness, and why you decided to build a round barn instead of the usual rectangular one, and what was the milk business like with horse-drawn carts? And then more deafness questions: what did you feel, going deaf? What was life like, in a silent world? I lived within a mile of my grandfather for twenty years, and I knew him quite well, yet I wish, I wish I had known him better.

I remember when I was in college sitting on the edge of his chair and scribbling to him, "I'm going to write a book for you and call it *The Round Barn*." He was pleased; but even coming that far I didn't make the leap and grab up more paper and begin asking then and there about the things that ought to go into the book. I guess it's because when you're young time seems so unlimited — there is plenty of time. Also, death is so uncomfortable. If you don't think about death, maybe it won't happen, at least not to anybody you care about.

But it did happen and then it was too late to get to know my grandfather in that special way. Too late to try to find out and understand *his* basic material. Years after, I began asking my grandmother about her childhood and other things, but I was too late there, too. She'd grown very old, and didn't remember.

Once, much earlier, some one of us kids did ask her how she met Grandpa. Grandma told us with relish, and Grandpa enjoyed watching our delighted faces, for he knew what story was being related. They'd both been college students, waiting on tables at a summer institute where adults, perhaps with their children, came in horse and buggy to live in one of the little cottages, eat in the common dining hall, enjoy the lake, and attend the concerts, lectures, and sermons. One evening Grandpa spilled a pat of butter off a tray and instead of picking it up he nudged it through a knothole in the floor with the toe of his shoe. Then he looked up with a merry Irish grin to see if anybody'd caught him in the act — and Grandma had. That was the instant she fell in love with him. But through the season Grandpa had another maiden besides Grandma who was making eyes at him. He couldn't decide between them. At summer's end he instructed each of the young ladies not to mail him any letters; he needed time to see how he felt, without pressure. But Grandma, lovesick, jumped the gun. She didn't *mail* a letter, she sent it by the hand of a mutual friend who was traveling from Appleton to the University of Wisconsin, where Grandpa was going to school. And when Grandpa read that letter, he was undone. The other girl didn't have a chance.

Every family has a few important stories everybody

knows; family legends. But even these will be lost, if they're not retold to each generation, and obviously they aren't — for where are the family legends of my great- and great-great-grandparents? I've never heard them.

When Demi was a baby she was given a baby book with a spot in it for her family tree. Her name, her two parents above, her four grandparents above them, her eight great-grandparents above them, branching ever more bushy the farther back it went, which is no doubt why genealogies are called family "trees." We filled in the blanks as best we could, and got pretty far back for certain lines of the family, but, with bare exceptions, beyond the grandparents they were all just names. Two of these exceptions were Demi's great-great-grandparents, Joseph and Maria Dale Trever, my great grandparents. My Great-Aunt Ria, fifth child in the Trever family (whom you met in the "Horrid" chapter when she asked my brother why he couldn't be a *good* little boy), wrote an account of their trip from England to America and the Mid West. An excerpt: "As soon as possible we left New York for Wisconsin. Our parents put us ten children on the train, then left us to buy food for this long journey. Someway, somehow, they misunderstood the time of the train's departure and they were not on board when the train pulled out. That was a cryin' time, I tell you for all of us! No mother, no father, no food! It turned out all right, however, as there was an express train which left the big city shortly after the departure of our train. Once our parents waved at us from their train as it passed ours. Later when we stopped at a station, they came joyfully aboard. What a happy reunion! After this, our first adventure in America, we could look out the windows and enjoy the sights, which we had seen before with tear-dimmed eyes and anxious thoughts."

What a treasure if there were at least one such story for

each of our ancestors, to lift him or her from the genealogi-
cal table and make him alive! We would be descended from
real people and not merely names on a chart. But how
many Aunt Ria's collected these stories and passed
them on?

My book *The Taste of Spruce Gum* came about because
of the stories of another person, an old person. I'd known
Vi Tuttle for ten Vermont summers but never paid much
attention to her, as young people mostly don't to old
people. Then one day I went with Vi's stepdaughter on an
excursion to a woolen mill, and we picked up Grandma Vi
in Rutland to go along, too. On the way we crossed
Shrewsbury Mountain. Eva said, "Oh Vi, tell Jackie some
of the stories of when you were a bride at the lumber camp
up here!"

So Vi began, in her dry Vermont style, and I listened
with half an ear and half a brain until suddenly I came to,
like a horse with a burr under his tail, for I finally realized
what I was hearing. I began listening eagerly. When she'd
pause I'd ask her a question to get her going again. She
talked all the way to the mill and back to Rutland, and
after we'd left her off I said, "All those stories would make
a fantastic book, if I only knew where to grab ahold of
them!"

It doesn't often happen this way to a writer or to anyone, but in the instant of exclaiming it, I *did* know — and
that sort of bolt-from-the-blue is one of the supreme joys
in life. I'd make Vi not a twenty-year-old bride but a
thirty-year-old widow, coming to marry a stranger, her
dead husband's brother. And the main character would be
a daughter who develops a violent hatred of her new stepfather. When I wrote the book I had to leave out some
stories Vi told about herself that would have been too
unbelievable with the change in her age. For instance, when
Vi first saw a birch tree she said, "How did they whitewash

that trunk up so far?" And when her chickens up at camp
— penned to save them from forest predators — began to
sicken and die, her husband asked, "What are you feeding
them?" She replied, "Feeding them? You don't have to
feed chickens." Of course you don't, back on an Illinois
farm where the chickens run free and gorge themselves
from the granaries, the cow and horse stalls, and alongside
the pig troughs! Though now that I reflect on it, I might
have made Libby, the child, display those ignorances. Well,
too late.

Anyway, off and on for the next several years I plied Vi
with questions. I got down everything I could about life
in the lumber camp and her attitude toward it. In the
process of building a story with all the details I had never
experienced myself — it might as well have been set in
1303 instead of 1903, for all the firsthand knowledge I had
of either era — I gradually learned what questions to ask.
You can guess them. They're the ones I've been asking you
throughout this book. The ones at the start of this chapter
that I wish I'd asked my grandfather.

To get the feel of the lumber camp I'd say to Grandma
Vi, "Stand on your veranda and tell me what you see"
— or smell — or hear. "Now go to the mill — the barn —
the woods — what was the drive up the mountain like? —
Christmas at Grandmother Bissell's?" And as Vi would
tell me details, she'd recall anecdotes, and I'd get these all
down. And when the anecdotes stopped coming, I'd nudge
her memory, often by imagining I was there myself, and
seeing where the blanks were: "What did you find to do,
all winter? Or on the long evenings? Weren't you lonely?
What did the shanty women do? How come Bert came to
Illinois and asked you to marry him? Did anything ever
frighten you at the camp? Make you miserable? Angry?"
One thing led to another and Vi kept talking, with both of
us enjoying it hugely.

A book I might have written, based on a real live source, never got past the idea. When we were living in Kent I heard about somebody's grandmother who had gone to work in a textile mill before there were labor laws to protect children from factory work. I was instantly interested. What was it like to earn your own living from seven years on? What was the factory like? How did she survive, working twelve, fourteen hours a day? Her stories would undoubtedly be grim, but there might possibly be touches of love, humor, even joy. But I didn't get around to hunting her up, and a year or so later I heard that she'd died.

However, I'm collecting my father's stories. If I hadn't asked about when he was a little boy, I wouldn't have heard of the time he was a painted Indian in Beloit's pageant for its seventy-fifth anniversary as a town. He spent the day running around with the other nine-year-old Indians, but feeling queerer and queerer, and when he was finally popped into the zinc bathtub (which his aunt never filled full enough for his satisfaction) the red wouldn't come off. He had the measles. Aunt Ida felt so sorry for Ronnie, in bed with his eyes covered, that she read him Batman out of the *Daily News* every day, even though she disapproved of such trash.

Or I wouldn't have heard how he carved his name on the inside of the boys' backhouse, at school, and after his little brother tattled on him his father led him across the fields, making him lug the heavy plane, and stood by while he wept and planed the whole board smooth. "Fools' names and fools' faces," said Grandpa sternly, and didn't that maxim get passed on to me as a child!

I'm finding out my mother's stories, too. She grew up in Chicago so her tales are set in a framework of blocks and sidewalks and trips down to the Loop on the El, and ballet and music classes at the American Conservatory. I'm glad the kids and I haven't missed hearing how the school bullies would halt her and her chum Hilda Duck and order them, "Dance!" Then the two small girls would have to hop up and down on the street corner and go through their steps, and if they slowed down the bullies would peg rocks at their feet. Or how she and Hilda and their classmates loved to eat their lunches in the warm school furnace room while the janitor heated up everybody's cocoa jugs in a large tub of hot water. Or about the curtained window they saw every day, behind which lay their friend Esther, dying of diabetes before the discovery of insulin.

Knowing more about my parents' lives helps me to understand my own life. I've come to talk much more openly with each of them about many vital things that affect me, in the present as well as the past. Equally important, it helps me to understand them; it deepens our relationship. I'm seeing my father, for instance, not just as my father but as a human being — a small boy; a young scamp giving his fraternity pin(s) to four different girls in the same day, then skipping off to a job in France and returning a year later, a responsible married man, with my mother. I'm seeing him as a middle-aged man, and now — well, as he put it in a letter to his seed dealers recently, explaining that he is retiring, "How does a kid get to be seventy next May?"

I think most people are willing to tell you their own stories. More than that, I think they're pleased, flattered, and delighted — but you may have some trouble getting them started. It's a challenge in many cases. What if they're too occupied to talk to you? Then you use an old technique of mine, which I call jumping on the bull walk.

That's a reference to a bull-exercising machine. We used to have one on the Dairy, a slatted movable track that went round and round, with stationary side rails, like a level escalator. The bull would be dragged up onto this — he never liked to exercise — by a stick that clamped onto a ring through his nose. He'd be tied there, the lever thrown, the track would start going around, and he'd have to walk in the same place until he'd had a sufficient workout. As kids we loved to start the bull walk. We'd walk and walk, all in a row, holding the rail. Once Patsy got her foot caught between the slats. With shrill screams she began to go around herself, and Joan, shrieking too, leapt to the lever just in time.

What I mean by this image that has anything to do with gathering stories, or really with just talking to anybody, is that if the person is on a bull walk, busy with his own occupations, you hop on, too. Follow him around, make comments, ask questions. If people are working with their hands, painting, cooking, patching a boat, digging a flower bed, repairing a motor, tramping through a corn field to see whether the blight has struck, they'll probably welcome company and conversation.

Actually, if I have to choose one method or the other, I prefer jumping on somebody's bull walk to having every-body stop for me and sit with folded hands. You can learn a lot while walking, painting, patching. I like to fit into on-going life, and have found that often enough I'm able to pull the lever myself, after a while, or at least fit the speed to my pace.

Look for other openings besides bull-walk ones. Take advantage of in-between spaces, such as gaps between one job and another, one place and another, one day and another. If the power goes off for an evening so the TV won't work, seize the moment. Light candles and talk. Long car rides are full of possibilities. Vacations are espe-cially fruitful, for then the ordinary schedule is broken. The family may sit around a camp fire, as we did in "Miseries," or visit old friends, a natural time for "do you remember when . . ." or "what ever happened to . . ." Holidays break the routine, too, and so do family festivals such as weddings, and even funerals. People are thrown out of their ruts, relatives often appear, and everyone might be more ready to talk.

Open times are frequently filled with problems and stresses on account of this. We're forced to quit hiding behind schedules and activities and may really notice each other for the first time in a long while. We may see things and say things which cause fights and friction, but we can also turn these to deep moments and happy encounters. Both are possible, even at the same time. And we will certainly learn something valuable.

Certain other times can be particularly rich for communication. When people are brought up short against the mysteries of life, and they realize how brief it is and how lonely we all are, then I've known them to reach out for communication and understanding. To switch off the TV and talk. TVitis is deadening not only in so much of what it gives us, but for what it deprives us of, such as the time and motivation to provide our own entertainment, including storytelling. Or the open space to get close to each other. But at times of grief, old age, illness, such space can open. It was when I visited my father in the hospital several years ago, with neither of us knowing whether he would recover, that I filled up three notebooks with the stories I've given you a pinch of. But I didn't do it by popping in and out and leaving a vase of flowers. I had to take time.

For it takes time and attention to talk to other people. You have to be willing to listen. It helps to be generous with your own stories, for these may prime the pump for someone else to be generous with hers or his. And remember that certain sorts of questions will usually get a response. "Did your family have enough to eat during the Depression?" "What did you do during the war?" "Did you ever get punished when you didn't deserve it?" "Why does Grandma make a face when she mentions Uncle Raymond?" You'll soon discover what the leading questions are, and you'll gain skill with practice.

One thing more. You have to be really interested. Your wanting to know will be what will make the most difference. For everybody has inner materials. Everybody has a story, many stories. Most people will never tell them, unless someone asks. Most won't think their stories are interesting or important, unless someone shows an interest. And practically none of these stories, even if they're told aloud, will ever get jotted down — unless you, Beloved Snail, do it.

Bibliography

B<small>IBLIOGRAPHIES AREN'T CHAPTERS.</small> They're usually alphabetical lists of the books and other materials the author used or referred to in writing the book, and they give all the publishing data about the materials so that you can go find them and read them if you want to. For this book, the bibliography is a list of all the books I've mentioned, but also some I haven't — and explaining why will turn this into a sort of chapter.

All summer, working on this manuscript, I've been interrupting the kids' reading and thoughts and conversation and activities to ask, "Who wrote such and such a book?" and, "There's a passage I want in *Caddie Wood-lawn*, Jill; will you find it for me?" and, "When are you going to pick out something from your journals that I can use?" So they haven't been unaware of this project. They've been in on it. (Also, when it's my turn to cook, my meals have been more slap-dash than theirs, and they comment on that, too.)

Anyway, last night one of my queries got them going on a discussion of some book — Phoebe and Coby, the campers in the "Miseries" chapter, are here, too — and they all decided to list some of their favorite books for me to include for you, books you might not ordinarily run across. So I grabbed a pencil and got down the titles, but not as much of the conversation as I'd have liked. The enthusiastic "yeahs" when someone mentioned a title, or the loud "no" from somebody, and then a collieshangie about the merits of that particular book.

Some of these I've already mentioned, but I'll give their list straight. For instance, Demi promptly began with *A Swarm in May*, and *Wind in the Willows*. Coby said the Tolkien trilogy: *The Lord of the Rings*, with *The Hobbit* as a preface. He's read the trilogy seven times or so, and has been a willing soulmate as I've just been reading the thousand-some pages for the first time, and have wanted to express my delight in the horrible spider, Shelob, and the orcs and Gollum and other characters. Jill's a Tolkien lover, too; she's memorizing the three-page poem in Elvish and has it posted in an appropriate place on the bathroom wall.

Then they all cried out, *Molesworth!* and I guess I'd better put back in the paragraph I cut out of the introduction:

I've always loved Latin and took a lot of it. But none of our girls has shown any interest in it, except in two books where Latin is part of the story: in *How to Be Topp*, Moles-worth tells how to be "topp" in Latin (we own four copies of this book because each girl wants her own; they recite chapters aloud by heart in the car), and in *A Swarm in May*, John Owen sings the stuff.

But there's lots more in *Swarm* and *Topp* than Latin.

The Potted Witch, by Vivian Scott, was recited in full, also by heart (with much expression on the *"Won't* you help your *poorrr* old mother with the dishes?"* and I do think Doubleday's missed a bet by letting that one go out of print so rapidly, and by not reviving it).

Phoebe brought up *Catch-22;* somebody *The Catcher in the Rye*, and Jill's read most of Kurt Vonnegut at thirteen. These are usually classed as "adult" books, but I don't make a fine distinction, and neither does this bunch. I like what C. S. Lewis said, "No work of the imagination is worth reading at the age of ten which is not equally (and often far more) worth reading at the age of fifty," and I know it often goes the other way: after all, many of the "classics" weren't written for kids, but were taken over by them. *Gulliver; Robinson Crusoe;* Mark Twain even de-clared that *Tom* and *Huck* weren't meant for children, but I think that was in reply to their being banned in some libraries as unfit for the young, shortly after their publication.

The *Tintin* and *Asterix* comic books were universally acclaimed, also *A High Wind in Jamaica*, and *Lord of the Flies*. (Discussion on how it compared with the movie.) Megan brought up *The Bronze Bow*. This made Jill recall another historical novel, *Warrior Scarlet*: "I only got it *half read* and you took it back to the *library* and then we *moved* and when am I ever going to get a chance to *finish it?*"

Megan, who owns two copies, recommended *The Little Prince*, which reminded Demi that she'd read *A Little*

Princess thirteen times, and that reminded everybody of *The Secret Garden*, also by Frances Hodgson Burnett, and *Little Lord Fauntleroy*.

Arthur Ransome got strong approval, especially *Winter Holiday, Swallowdale*, and *Swallows and Amazons*. ("Some of his books aren't quite so good, like *Missee Lee*, but they're *all* better than *most* books.")

Jill mentioned a picture book, *The Giving Tree*, which last year, at their advanced ages, caused her and Demi to burst into tears, and Megan to depart rapidly from the kitchen so that she wouldn't, but that's a story worth a couple of pages. Two books I haven't read, *Diamond in the Window* and *Swing in the Summerhouse*, came next, "even better than the *Green Knowe* books," so I'd better read them, and from Megan: Paul Berna and *One Hundred Thousand Francs*. And how about Alan Garner and *The Moon of Gomrath*, somebody interrupted, and, "Oh — we're forgetting *Harriet the Spy!*"

"What's that one with birds in the title?" was identified as *Linnets and Valerians*, and then a quick approval of all Elizabeth Goudge's books, especially *The Little White Horse*. Then *Cloud Forest*, and two recent Atlantic–Little, Brown publications: *Moon Eyes*, and *A Room Made of Windows*. (There's a payoff for you, Editors, for keeping us supplied with reading!) C. S. Lewis's *Narnia* series — much discussion on which of the seven was best. Somebody didn't like *The Last Battle* at all, and somebody else liked it better than the others — and then Demi mentioned *Moomintroll* and all faces lit up and voices got soft and loving — oh yeah — of course — how could we forget them — Snufkin — and Sniff — (long argument on which episode is in which book) — and the Snork Maiden . . .

(Me writing furiously and enjoying all this.)

"*Elsie Dinsmore!*" cries Jill, and everybody laughs and groans, "and the forty sequels!" and "Elsie's so awful, she's great," and Megan says to me, "Tell 'em to read *old* books!"

Then came *Jane Eyre* and *Animal Farm* ("Yeah." "Ick."), and *Winnie the Pooh*, and "*Miss Bianca*'s okay," and the talk trickled off and interest shifted, and I asked Megan to make me some cinnamon toast, too, since she was making it for herself.

Writing this up from my notes, a couple months later, I wonder where Elspeth was. Well, it must have been nothing serious, for she's here now, and fine. Also, this is by no means a complete list of well-loved books. If the idea had hit on another night, there would have been other titles, though I think there is a core of reading from these kids which would be mentioned any night. One real omission, though, is Eleanor Farjeon. Demi and I were repairing a step together one evening shortly after this discussion, and while we were resting from the sawing and hammering she said, "I think Eleanor Farjeon more than any other writer has made me not afraid to grow old." I wished with all my heart that Eleanor Farjeon were still alive, so that I could have written that tribute to her.

So on to the formal bibliography. It's in alphabetical order, and I'll do it by putting the author first, which is proper, but if a title has been mentioned anywhere in the book without its author in tow (or in fills!), that title will be listed, too. Where I can, I will put the date of the original publication in, right after the title, especially in the case of old books; if I haven't listed a recent date on any book it still may be available, even popular, in hardcover or paperback. I know you can get *Goops*, right now, from Dover.

Abbe, Patience, Richard and John, *Around the World in Eleven Years*, Stokes, 1936.

Aldrich, Thomas, *The Story of a Bad Boy* (1870), Pantheon, 1951.
Alice's Adventures in Wonderland, see Carroll, Lewis.
Alone on an Island, see Dell, Heather.
American Diaries, see Matthews, William.
The Animal Family, see Jarrell, Randall.
Animal Farm, see Orwell, George.
An Anteater Named Arthur, see Waber, Bernard.
Appleton, Victor, *see* Stratemeyer, Edward.
Arbuthnot, May Hill, and S. L. Root, eds., *Time for Poetry*, Scott, Foresman, 1961.
Asterix, *see* Goscinny and Uderzo.
At the Back of the North Wind, see Macdonald, George.

Barrie, Sir James, *Sentimental Tommy* (1896), Scribner, 1918.
A Window in Thrums (1889), Dodd, Mead, 1896.
Baum, L. Frank, *The Wizard of Oz* (1900), Dover reprint, 1960.
Belloc, Hilaire, *Cautionary Tales for Children* (1908) is a unified edition with other Belloc books called *Cautionary Verses*, Knopf, 1968.
Berger, Josef, *Small Voices*, Eriksson, 1966.
Berna, Paul, *One Hundred Thousand Francs.* The American edition is called *The Horse Without a Head*, Pantheon, 1958.
The Blue Bird, see Maeterlinck, Maurice.
The Book of Maggie Owen, see Wadelton, Maggie-Owen.
Boston, Lucy, *The River at Green Knowe*, Harcourt Brace, 1959; *The Treasure of Green Knowe* (called *The Chimneys of Green Knowe* in the English edition), Harcourt Brace, 1958.
Boswell, James. Many volumes of Boswell's journals have been published. You might begin with *Boswell's London Journal, 1762–1763*, McGraw-Hill, 1963.
A Boy of the Lost Crusade, see Hewes, Agnes D.
Brand, Christianna, ed., *Naughty Children*, Dutton, 1963.
Bread and Jam for Frances, see Hoban, Russell.
Brink, Carol Ryrie, *Caddie Woodlawn*, Macmillan, 1935.
British and Scottish Diaries, see Matthews, William.
Brontë, Charlotte, *Jane Eyre* (1847), World, 1946.
The Bronze Bow, see Speare, Elizabeth.
Buckeridge, Anthony, *Jennings Goes to School*, Collins, 1950.

Burgess, Gelett, *Goops and How to Be Them: A Manual of Manners for Polite Infants*, Lippincott, 1900; *More Goops and How Not to Be Them*, Lippincott, 1903.

Burnett, Frances Hodgson, *Little Lord Fauntleroy* (1886), Dent Children's Illustrated Classics, 1962; *A Little Princess* (1888), as *Sara Crewe; Or, What Happened at Miss Minchin's*, Lippincott, 1963; *The Secret Garden* (1911), Lippincott, 1962.

Caddie Woodlawn, see Brink, Carol Ryrie.

Cameron, Eleanor, *A Room Made of Windows*, Atlantic–Little, Brown, 1971.

Carroll, Lewis, *Alice's Adventures in Wonderland* (1865) and *Through the Looking Glass* (1871). Many editions, both books often published together. A good paperback is Signet CD 22; a volume that will tell you a lot is *The Annotated Alice*, with introduction and notes by Martin Gardner, Clarkson Potter, 1960. "The Lobster-Quadrille" is in *Wonderland;* "The Walrus and the Carpenter" and "Jabberwocky" are in *Looking Glass.*

Catch-22, see Heller, Joseph.

The Catcher in the Rye, see Salinger, J. D.

Centennial Book of Beloit, 1936. Could undoubtedly be found in the Beloit, Wisconsin, public library. Our copy is mislaid. (Whoops! My mother found theirs. It's *The Book of Beloit*, published in 1936 by the Daily News Publishing Company on the occasion of the One Hundredth Anniversary of the arrival of the first settlers at the junction of the Turtle and the Rock, where the Beloit of today is a monument to their courage and their initiative.)

Charlotte's Web, see White, E. B.

Chase, Richard, *The Jack Tales*, Houghton Mifflin, 1943.

The Chatterlings, see Lipman, Michael.

The Chimneys of Green Knowe, see Boston, Lucy.

Cloud Forest, see North, Joan.

Cole, William, ed., *Beastly Boys and Ghastly Girls*, World, 1971.

Cornford, Frances, "The Watch," is from *Collected Poems*, Cresset Press, Ltd., 1954.

cummings, e.e. The phrases on page 134 are from Chansons Innocents, I, "in Just-spring," from *Tulips and Chimneys*

(1923) and can be found in *The Complete Poems 1913–1962*, Harcourt Brace, 1972.

Defoe, Daniel, *Robinson Crusoe* (1719–1720), Oxford, 1973.
de la Mare, Walter, *Collected Poems, 1901–1918*, Holt, 1920. The complete "Miss T." is also found in Arbuthnot and Root, *Time for Poetry*.
Dell, Heather, *Alone on an Island*, unpublished.
Diamond in the Window, see Langton, Jane.
Dickens, Charles, *Oliver Twist* (1837–39; published serially), many editions, many paperback.
Dixon, Franklin, *see* Stratemeyer, Edward.
Duff, Annis, *Bequest of Wings* (1944), revised edition, Viking, 1954.

The Education of H*Y*M*A*N K*A*P*L*A*N, *see* Rosten, Leo.
Edwards, Dorothy, *My Naughty Little Sister*, Methuen, 1952.
Eliot, T. S., "Old Possum's Book of Practical Cats" (1939) may be found in *T. S. Eliot, The Complete Poems and Plays, 1909–1950*, Harcourt Brace, 1952.
Elsie Dinsmore, see Finley, Martha.

Farjeon, Eleanor, "Girls' Names" and "Boys' Names" are from *Over the Garden Wall*, Lippincott, 1933. Read also *The Little Bookroom*, Oxford University Press, 1955, and *Martin Pippin in the Daisy Field* (1937), Puffin, 1966.
Finley, Martha, *Elsie Dinsmore* (1867), Dodd, Mead, 1893.
Fitzhugh, Louise, *Harriet the Spy*, Harper & Row, 1964.
Frank, Anne, *Anne Frank: The Diary of a Young Girl*, Doubleday, 1952.
Frost, Robert. The poems "The Pasture" and "Stopping by Woods on a Snowy Evening" can both be found in *You Come Too*, Holt, Rinehart, and Winston, 1959. "Departmental," in the same book, contains the discussion of the ant, Jerry McCormic.

Garner, Alan, *The Moon of Gomrath*, Walck, 1967.
Gibbons, Euell, *Stalking the Wild Asparagus*, McKay, 1962.
Gibson, William, *The Miracle Worker*, Knopf, 1957.

The Giving Tree, see Silverstein, Shel.

Golding, William, *The Lord of the Flies,* Coward-McCann, 1962.

Goops and How To Be Them, see Burgess, Gelett.

Goscinny, René de, and Uderzo, the Asterix series. These hard-cover "comics" take place in 50 B.C. Start with *Asterix the Gaul,* Brockhampton, 1969 (published originally in French in 1961).

Goudge, Elizabeth, *Linnets and Valerians,* Brockhampton, 1964; *The Little White Horse,* Brockhampton, 1946.

Grahame, Kenneth, *The Wind in the Willows* (1908), Scribner, 1933, and numerous paperback editions.

Green Eggs and Ham, see Dr. Seuss.

Gulliver's Travels, see Swift, Jonathan.

The Happy Mother Goose; Jolly Versions of Nursery Favorites: Nursery Rhymes for Today's Child. Original concept by Geoffrey Hall, 1950. I have been unable to locate the publisher. I understand there was a Victor recording of these by Kukla, Fran and Ollie.

Hardy Boys, see Stratemeyer, Edward.

Harriet the Spy, see Fitzhugh, Louise.

Harris, Joel Chandler, *Uncle Remus* (1883), Gale (Singing Tree), 1971, and numerous editions and paperbacks.

Hawthorne, Nathaniel, *A Wonder Book* (1851), Dutton, Children's Illustrated Classics, no date [1927].

Heller, Joseph, *Catch-22,* Simon & Schuster, 1961.

Heller, Suzanne, *Misery for Everybody* (selected cartoons from *Misery, More Misery,* and *Misery Loves Company*), Fawcett, 1970.

Hergé (French author/artist of the Tintin hard-cover "comic" books). Titles include *The Crab with the Golden Claws, The Secret of the Unicorn, Tintin in Tibet, The Castafiore Emerald* (my favorite), and many others. Translated into nine or more languages. English editions available from Methuen and Atlantic–Little, Brown.

Hewes, Agnes D., *A Boy of the Lost Crusade,* Houghton Mifflin, 1923.

A High Wind in Jamaica, see Hughes, Richard A.

Hoban, Russell, *Bread and Jam for Frances*, Harper & Row, 1964.
The Hobbit, see Tolkien, J. R. R.
Hoffmann, Heinrich, *Struwwelpeter* (translated, 1844), Routledge & Kegan Paul, Ltd., no date.
Homer, *The Iliad, The Odyssey*. An excellent retelling that contains both epics is *The Children's Homer*, by Padraic Colum, Macmillan, 1918.
How to Be Topp, see Willans, Geoffrey, and Searle, Ronald.
Hudson, Virginia Cary, *O Ye Jigs & Juleps*, Macmillan, 1962.
Hughes, Richard A., *A High Wind in Jamaica* (1928), Harper, 1957.

"In the squdgy river," is from "The Hippopotamus" by Georgia Roberts Durston; see Arbuthnot, May Hill, and S. L. Root, *Time for Poetry*, Scott, Foresman, 1961.

Jack and Jill, a current magazine for children, published in Philadelphia.
Jackson, Jacqueline. My books, in publication order: *Julie's Secret Sloth*, Little, Brown, 1953; *The Paleface Redskins*, Little, Brown, 1958; *The Taste of Spruce Gum*, Little, Brown, 1966; *Missing Melinda*, Little, Brown, 1967; *Chicken Ten Thousand*, Little, Brown, 1968; *The Ghost Boat*, Little, Brown, 1969; *Spring Song*, Kent State University Press, 1969; *The Orchestra Mice*, Reilly & Lee, 1970; *The Endless Pavement* (with William Perlmutter), Seabury, 1973; *Turn Not Pale, Beloved Snail*, Little, Brown, 1974.
Jane Eyre, see Brontë, Charlotte.
Jansson, Tove, author of the *Moomintroll* series. Try starting with *Finn Family Moomintroll*, Walck, 1965; also *Tales from Moominvalley*, Walck, 1964.
Jarrell, Randall, *The Animal Family*, Pantheon, 1965.
Jennings Goes to School, see Buckeridge, Anthony.
"Johari Window." This concept was developed by two psychologists, Joseph Luft and Harry Ingraham, and "johari" is a combination of their names, not some esoteric Eastern word! You can read more about it in Luft, Joseph, *Of Human Interaction*, National Press, 1961.

Juster, Norton, *The Phantom Tollbooth*, Random House, 1961.
Just So Stories, see Kipling, Rudyard.

Keller, Helen, *The Story of My Life*, Doubleday, 1964. I haven't
been able to find any data on *Three Days to See*.
Kingsley, Charles, *The Heroes* (1856), Dutton, Children's Illus-
trated Classics; *The Waterbabies* (1863), Dutton, Children's
Illustrated Classics.
Kipling, Rudyard, *Just So Stories* (1902), Schocken, 1965.
Kroeber, Theodora, *Ishi in Two Worlds*, University of California
Press, 1961; *Ishi, Last of His Tribe*, Parnassus, 1964.
Krumgold, Joseph, . . . *and Now Miguel*, Crowell, 1953; *Onion
John*, Crowell, 1959; *Henry Three*, Atheneum, 1967.

Langton, Jane, *Diamond in the Window*, Harper & Row, 1962;
The Swing in the Summerhouse, Harper & Row, 1967.
Lewis, C. S. The Chronicles of Narnia comprise seven books:
The Lion, the Witch and the Wardrobe (1950); *Prince Caspian*
(1951); *The Voyage of the Dawn Treader* (1952); *The Silver
Chair* (1953); *The Horse and His Boy* (1954); *The Magician's
Nephew* (1955); and *The Last Battle* (1956). You can get them
all boxed together in paperback from Collier-Macmillan, 1970.
Linnets and Valerians, see Goudge, Elizabeth.
Lipman, Michael, *The Chatterlings*, Volland, 1928.
Liske, Louisa, *The Touching Book,* unpublished.
Little Lord Fauntleroy, see Burnett, Frances Hodgson.
The Little Prince, see Saint-Exupéry, Antoine de.
A Little Princess, see Burnett, Frances Hodgson.
Lofting, Hugh, *The Story of Doctor Doolittle*, Lippincott, 1920.
Lord of the Flies, see Golding, William.
The Lord of the Rings, see Tolkien, J. R. R.
Lorenz, Konrad, *King Solomon's Ring*, Crowell, 1952.

Mabie, Hamilton Wright, *Folk Tales Every Child Should Know*,
Doubleday, 1910.
Macdonald, George, *At the Back of the North Wind* (1871),
Macmillan, 1964; *The Princess and Curdie* (1883), Macmillan,
1954; *The Princess and the Goblin* (1872), Macmillan, 1967.

Maeterlinck, Maurice, *The Blue Bird*, Dodd, Mead, 1909. Originally a play, put in book form by the author's wife.
Maggie No Doubt, see Wadelton, Maggie-Owen.
Mary Poppins, see Travers, Pamela.
Matthews, William, *American Diaries, an Annotated Bibliography of Diaries Written Prior to the Year 1861*, Canner, 1959 (reproduction of 1945 edition); *American Diaries in Manuscript*, University of Georgia Press, 1973. *British and Scottish Diaries* I was unable to find any data on, but there is a *British Diaries* by the above author, R. West, 1973 (reproduction of 1950 edition), and *British Diaries Annotated, 1442–1492*, Peter Smith, no date.
Mayne, William, *A Swarm in May*, Oxford University Press, 1955.
Millay, Edna St. Vincent. "The Ballad of the Harp-Weaver" is from *The Harp-Weaver and Other Poems*, Harper, 1922.
Milne, A. A., *Winnie the Pooh*, Dutton, 1926. The poem "Hoppity" is from *When We Were Very Young*, Dutton, 1924.
Milton, John, *Paradise Lost* (1667). Many editions, try Christopher Ricks, ed., New American Library, 1968.
The Miracle Worker, see Gibson, William.
Miss Bianca, see Sharp, Margery.
"Miss T.," *see* de la Mare, Walter.
Moomintroll books, *see* Jansson, Tove.
Moon Eyes, see Poole, Josephine.
Moore, John, *You English Words: A Book About Them*, Lippincott, 1961.
My Baby Brother, see Scarry, Patsy.
My Naughty Little Sister, see Edwards, Dorothy.

Narnia Chronicles, *see* Lewis, C. S.
Naughty Children, see Brand, Christianna.
Neville, Mary, *Woody and Me*, Pantheon, 1966.
North, Joan, *Cloud Forest*, Farrar, Straus & Giroux, 1965.

O Ye Jigs & Juleps, see Hudson, Virginia Cary.
Oliver Twist, see Dickens, Charles.
Orwell, George, *Animal Farm*, Harcourt Brace Jovanovich, 1954. New American Library (paperback), 1971.

The Oxford English Dictionary. The 1933 edition runs to thirteen magnificent volumes. In 1971 the Clarendon Press brought out a complete *OED* in two volumes, including a magnifying glass.

Parmenter, Ross, *The Awakened Eye*, Wesleyan University Press, 1968.

Pepys, Samuel, *The Diary of Samuel Pepys.* Kept in code from 1660 to 1669, decoded about one hundred years later and published in 1825. Many editions. Try *The Diary of Samuel Pepys* (selections), O. F. Morshead, ed., Harper Torchbooks, 1960.

Pepys's Diary, *see* Pepys, Samuel.

Peter Rabbit, *see* Potter, Beatrix.

The Phantom Tollbooth, see Juster, Norton.

Poole, Josephine, *Moon Eyes*, Atlantic–Little, Brown, 1967.

Potok, Chaim, *The Chosen*, Simon & Schuster, 1967.

Potter, Beatrix, *The Tale of Peter Rabbit*, Warne, 1902. The word "toothsome" *isn't* in *The Tale of Mrs. Tittlemouse*, and I can't for the life of me track down where in Potter it is.

The Princess and Curdie, see Macdonald, George.

Ransome, Arthur, *Missee Lee*, Cape, 1941; *Swallows and Amazons*, Cape, 1930; *Winter Holiday*, Cape, 1933.

The River at Green Knowe, see Boston, Lucy.

Robinson Crusoe, see Defoe, Daniel.

A Room Made of Windows, see Cameron, Eleanor.

Rosten, Leo, *The Education of H*Y*M*A*N K*A*P*L*A*N*, Harcourt Brace, 1937. (Written under the pseudonym Leonard Q. Ross.) Try also *The Joys of Yiddish*, McGraw-Hill, 1968.

Saint-Exupéry, Antoine de, *The Little Prince*, Harcourt Brace, 1946.

Salinger, J. D., *The Catcher in the Rye*, Little, Brown, 1951.

Saturday Review–World, a magazine that often deals with word fun.

Scarry, Patsy, *My Baby Brother*, Simon & Schuster, 1956.

Schulz, Charles, *Happiness Is a Warm Puppy*, Rand, 1971; *Security Is a Thumb and a Blanket*, Rand, 1971.

Scott, Vivian, *The Potted Witch*, Harcourt Brace, 1957.

The Secret Garden, see Burnett, Frances Hodgson.

Sendak, Maurice, *Where the Wild Things Are*, Harper & Row, 1963.

Seuss, Dr., *Green Eggs and Ham*, Random House, 1960.

Sharp, Margery, *Miss Bianca*, Little, Brown, 1962.

Silverstein, Shel, *The Giving Tree*, Harper & Row, 1964.

Small Voices, see Berger, Josef.

Speare, Elizabeth, *The Bronze Bow*, Houghton Mifflin, 1961.

Stevenson, Robert Louis, *A Child's Garden of Verses* (1883), World, 1946.

Stokes, Jack, *Wiley and the Hairy Man*, Macrae, 1970.

Storr, Catherine, *Marianne Dreams*, Faber and Faber, 1958.

The Story of Doctor Doolittle, see Lofting, Hugh.

Stratemeyer, Edward. Here's a lulu. This man started a syndicate in 1908 to grind out children's books, and it's still going. He and the syndicate used many pseudonyms. As Franklin Dixon, he (or they) wrote *The Hardy Boys;* as Laura Lee Hope, *The Bobbsey Twins;* as Victor Appleton, *Tom Swift and His Aerial Warship* (typical Tom Swift titles are now *Tom Swift, Jr. and His Electronic Retroscope*); as Carolyn Keene, the *Nancy Drew* books; as Arthur Winfield, the *Rover Boys;* and many more names for many more series. I believe Grosset & Dunlap was and is publisher for all these. I'm wondering how I can join up.

Struwwelpeter, see Hoffman, Heinrich.

Sutcliffe, Rosemary, *Warrior Scarlet* (1958), Walck, 1966.

Swallowdale, see Ransome, Arthur.

A Swarm in May, see Mayne, William.

Swift, Jonathan, *Gulliver's Travels* (1726), available in many editions, usually edited for children, good parts cut out.

The Swing in the Summerhouse, see Langton, Jane.

Tales from Moominvalley, see Jansson, Tove.

Taylor, Theodore, *The Cay*, Doubleday, 1969.

Tennyson, Alfred, Lord. We have "Idyls of the King" (1858); "Ulysses" (1842) and "Break, Break, Break" (1842) in a volume, *Tennyson's Poems*, National Library Association, 1891, which Elspeth just spilled apple juice all over. But that's all right, just last week she rescued one called simply *Tennyson,*

Crowell, 1885, from her school's garbage bin. I memorized "The Lady of Shalott" from the former copy when I was twelve.

Through the Looking Glass, see Carroll, Lewis.

Thurber, James, *The Thirteen Clocks*, Simon & Schuster, 1950; *The Wonderful O*, Simon & Schuster, 1957.

Tintin, see Hergé.

Tolkien, J. R. R., *The Hobbit*, Houghton Mifflin, 1938; *The Lord of the Rings* (published in England, 1954–56), Houghton Mifflin, 1965.

Tom Swift, detour by Victor Appleton or else go directly to Stratemeyer, Edward.

Travers, Pamela L., *Mary Poppins* (1934), Harcourt, Brace, World, 1934.

The Treasure of Green Knowe, see Boston, Lucy.

Twain, Mark, *A Connecticut Yankee in King Arthur's Court* (1889); *Huckleberry Finn* (1884); *Tom Sawyer* (1876). Many modern editions, including paperbacks. Beware of abridgements and adaptations.

Uncle Remus, see Harris, Joel Chandler.

Vonnegut, Kurt. Some of his books are *Cat's Cradle*, Delacourt, 1963; *God Bless You, Mr. Rosewater*, Delacourt, 1965; *Welcome to the Monkey House*, Delacourt, 1950. Available in paperback through Dell.

Waber, Bernard, *An Anteater Named Arthur*, Houghton Mifflin, 1967.

Wadelton, Maggie-Owen, *The Book of Maggie Owen*, Bobbs-Merrill, 1941; *Maggie No Doubt*, Bobbs-Merrill, 1943.

Warrior Scarlet, see Sutcliffe, Rosemary.

The Waterbabies, see Kingsley, Charles.

Where the Wild Things Are, see Sendak, Maurice.

White, E. B., *Charlotte's Web*, Harper & Row, 1952.

Wier, Ester, *The Loner*, McKay, 1963.

Wilder, Laura Ingalls, *By the Shores of Silver Lake*, Harper,

1939; *On the Banks of Plum Creek,* Harper, 1937. Don't miss any Wilder books.

Wiley and the Hairy Man, see Stokes, Jack.

Willans, Geoffrey, and Searle, Ronald, *How to Be Topp,* Parrish, 1954.

The Wind in the Willows, see Grahame, Kenneth.

A Window in Thrums, see Barrie, Sir James.

Winnie the Pooh, see Milne, A. A.

The Wizard of Oz, see Baum, L. Frank.

So, there's the list. Making a bibliography is a gigantic job, I've discovered. But really fun, a detective search, and it sure teaches you to use the reference room of the library. (That bit on Stratemeyer was in a dictionary of pseudonyms. Who'd ever think there'd be a book like that?) I hope I haven't missed any entries; I've surely made some mistakes and I apologize if I lead you astray.

But one last thing. I bet you've forgotten that I said in "Gerk" I'd tell you what Prince Tip o' Tongue's crown-winning words were, the two that meant exactly the same thing, in *The Chatterlings.* But *I* haven't. And here they are. I admit that from age seven on I had a lingering suspicion that they were a bit of a cheat, that the second word wasn't a jolly old legitimate English one — who uses it? But it's okay, I just looked it up in the OED, and the pair stands:

END   FINIS

Acknowledgments

Selections from the book were taped and aired between 1969 and 1974 on WHA School of the Air at the University of Wisconsin.

"How (Maybe) to Write a Children's Book" appeared in *Publishers Weekly*, February 1972.

"How (Maybe) to Write a Children's Book" was reprinted from *Publishers Weekly* in *The Writer*, April 1974.

Grateful acknowledgment is made to the following publishers and individuals, for permission to reprint copyrighted material in this book.